TURKEY EXPLORATION & TRAVEL GUIDE

Turkey

MATTHEW CELEBI

COPYRIGHT

CONTENTS

CONTENTS 4

INTRODUCTION 7

Turkey 7

CHAPTER 1 15

Turkey Unveiled 15

History of Turkey 16

Geography 19

Climate 21

Language and Communication Tips 23

Religion and Cultural Etiquette 25

Festivals and Celebrations 26

Top Reasons to Visit 33

CHAPTER 2 39

Planning Your Trip to Turkey 39

Best Time to Explore Turkey 40

Essential Items to Pack 43

Visa and Insurance Requirements for Turkey 49

Transportation Options to Turkey 54

CHAPTER 3 61

ISTANBUL 61

Best Areas to Stay in Istanbul.................................63

Best Hotels to Stay in Istanbul 66

Best Places to Visit in Istanbul 70

Best Restaurants in Istanbul 75

Best Shopping Centers in Istanbul......................79

Nightlife in Istanbul.......................................83

Exploring Istanbul in 7 Days 86

CHAPTER 4...93

ANTALYA...93

Best Areas to Stay in Antalya............................94

Best Hotels to Stay in Antalya 97

Best Places to Visit in Antalya 100

Best Restaurants in Antalya 106

Best Shopping Centers in Antalya......................110

Nightlife in Antalya 114

Exploring Antalya in 7 Days 118

CHAPTER 5...124

IZMIR 124

Best Areas to Stay in Izmir...............................124

Best Hotels to Stay in Izmir Luxury Hotels 128

Best Restaurants in Izmir 135

Best Places to visit in Izmir 141

Nightlife In Izmir 145

CHAPTER 6..149

CAPPADOCIA 149

Best Areas to Stay in Cappadocia.......................149

Best Hotels in Cappadocia 153

Best Place to Stay in Cappadocia........................156

Best Resturants in Cappadocia 160

Best Places to visit in Cappadocia.......................163

Nightlife in Cappadocia 167

CHAPTER 7..171

MUSEUMS, HISTORY, AND HIDDEN GEMS IN TURKEY..171

CHAPTER 8..177

MUST TRY FOOOD IN TURKEY. 177

CHAPTER 9..188

Travel Tips for Exploring Turkey 188

CHAPTER 10...192

10 DAYS ITINERARY IN TURKEY 192

CHAPTER 11...197

FACTS ABOUT TURKEY....................................197

Fun Trivia About Turkey 198

CONCLUSION 199

The Journey, The Discovery, The Adventure.................200

INTRODUCTION
Turkey

Did you know that Istanbul is the only city in the world that spans two continents, Europe and Asia?

This extraordinary fact is a perfect introduction to Turkey—a country that bridges not just two continents but also thousands of years of history, diverse cultures, and stunning natural landscapes. With a foot in both East and West, Turkey is a land of contrasts and harmony, a place where ancient ruins coexist with modern skylines, and traditional bazaars hum alongside vibrant cityscapes.

From the glittering waters of the Bosphorus to the surreal landscapes of Cappadocia, Turkey offers something for everyone. It's a nation of storytellers, where every stone, street, and spice tell a tale of resilience, transformation, and cultural richness. Let's journey into this fascinating land and uncover why Turkey is not just a destination—it's an experience.

Country: Turkey

Continent: Europe and Asia

Capital: Ankara

Currency: Turkish Lira (TRY)

Official Language: Turkish

Major Cities: Istanbul, Ankara, Izmir, Antalya, Bursa

Most Prominent Landmarks: Hagia Sophia, Blue Mosque, Ephesus, Cappadocia, Pamuk kale, Mount Nem rut, Tokai Palace

Date of Establishment: October 29, 1923 (Proclamation of the Republic of Turkey)

Population: Approximately 85 million (2023)

Size: 302,455 square miles (783,356 square kilometers)

Nickname(s): Bridge Between Continents, Land of Four Seasons

Motto: "Gemelli, kyats şartsız Millender" (Sovereignty unconditionally belongs to the Nation)

National Anthem: "Itkila Maris" (Independence March)

National Flower: Tulip

National Bird: Redwing (Turdus iliacus)

Postal Code: Typically, 5 digits, e.g., 06010

Country Code: +90

Time Zone: Turkey Time (TRT), UTC+3

Plug Type: Type C and Type F (two round prongs)

Leading Industries: Tourism, Automotive, Textiles, Agriculture, Electronics, Construction

Transportation: Buses, Metro systems, Domus (shared minibuses), High-speed trains, Ferries

Main Airports: Istanbul Airport (IST), Sabiha Gökçen International Airport (SAW), Antalya Airport (AYT), Ankara Sambora Airport (ESB)

Fun Fact: Istanbul is the only city in the world that spans two continents, Europe and Asia.

Turkey's geographical position is nothing short of extraordinary. Most of the country lies in Anatolia, nestled in West Asia, while a smaller but significant portion, East Thrace, sits in Southeast Europe. This unique position means Turkey borders an array of nations and seas: the Black Sea to the north, the Aegean Sea to the west, and the Mediterranean to the south. Sharing borders with countries as varied as Greece, Iran, and Syria, Turkey's landscape mirrors its cultural diversity.

Home to over 85 million people, Turkey is a vibrant mosaic of ethnicities and traditions. While the majority of the population identifies as ethnic Turks, the Kurdish community represents the largest minority, contributing richly to the country's culture. Although officially a secular state, Turkey is predominantly Muslim, a fact reflected in its architecture, customs, and daily rhythms. Yet, the spirit of secularism shines in its capital, Ankara, and its bustling metropolis, Istanbul—Turkey's largest city and financial heart.

Turkey's story begins thousands of years ago, in the Late Paleolithic era, when modern humans first roamed its lands. This ancient soil is home to some of humanity's earliest milestones. Sites like Gabelli Tepe—believed to be the world's oldest temple—stand as testaments to Turkey's role as a cradle of civilization. Here, agriculture took root, and communities flourished, giving rise to the Hittites, a powerful ancient Anatolian people.

As the centuries passed, Turkey became a melting pot of cultures. With the conquests of Alexander, the Great, Anatolia transitioned into a Hellenistic hub, where Greek culture mingled with local traditions. This period of cultural fusion continued under Roman and Byzantine rule, leaving behind awe-inspiring monuments like the Hagia Sophia and the ancient city of Ephesus.

The arrival of the Seljuk Turks in the 11th century marked a turning point, initiating the Turkification of Anatolia. Later, the Ottoman Empire, founded in 1299, transformed Turkey into a global power. Under the leadership of figures like Mehmed the Conqueror and Suleiman the Magnificent, the Ottomans expanded their influence, leaving an indelible mark on the world. Even today, Turkey's rich heritage reflects the grandeur of its Ottoman past.

Fast forward to the early 20th century, and Turkey underwent another dramatic transformation. Following the fall of the Ottoman Empire and the devastation of World War I, the Turkish War of Independence gave birth to the Republic of Turkey in 1923. Led by Mustafa Kemal Atatürk, the new republic embraced sweeping reforms, modernizing its institutions and embracing a secular identity.

Today, Turkey is a vibrant democracy with a growing economy. It plays a key role on the global stage, from its membership in NATO to its position as an emerging regional power. Yet, amidst this modernity, Turkey remains deeply connected to its past, blending ancient traditions with contemporary aspirations.

Turkey's geography is as diverse as its history. From the rugged mountains of the east to the fertile plains of the west, every corner of Turkey offers a unique landscape. The central plateau, known as Anatolia, is the country's heartland, while coastal plains stretch along its three major seas.

The climate, too, varies dramatically. The coasts enjoy a Mediterranean climate with hot summers and mild winters, making them ideal for beach lovers. In contrast, the interior experiences harsher conditions, with cold winters and scorching summers. Whether you're exploring the snowy peaks of Mount Ararat or basking on the beaches of Antalya, Turkey's natural beauty never fails to amaze.

Turkey is a treasure trove of cultural heritage. With 21 UNESCO World Heritage sites and 30 UNESCO intangible cultural heritage inscriptions, it's a haven for history buffs and culture enthusiasts. Marvel at the intricate carvings of the ancient city of Troy, walk through the otherworldly travertine terraces of Pamuk kale, or lose yourself in the fairy chimneys of Cappadocia.

The country's rich traditions extend to its vibrant festivals, lively bazaars, and culinary delights. Turkish cuisine is a celebration of flavors, from the savory kebabs of Gaziantep to the sweet indulgence of baklava. And let's not forget the cultural rituals of tea and coffee—symbols of hospitality and connection in Turkish society.

One of Turkey's most striking features is its ability to blend contrasts seamlessly. Istanbul, for example, is a city where ancient mosques and Byzantine churches coexist with modern skyscrapers and chic boutiques. This juxtaposition of old and new is reflected throughout the country, creating a dynamic yet harmonious atmosphere.

Beyond its cities, Turkey offers a range of experiences for every traveler. Adventure seekers can hike through the rugged Kakkar Mountains, history enthusiasts can explore the ruins of Ephesus, and sunseekers can relax on the beaches of Bodrum. No matter your interests, Turkey has something to offer.

So, why visit Turkey? The reasons are as varied as the country itself. It's a place where you can stand in awe of ancient history one moment and sip Turkish tea in a bustling bazaar the next. It's a destination where natural wonders like the hot air balloons of Cappadocia and the turquoise waters of Loudened take your breath away. And it's a country where every interaction, from sharing a meal to wandering its streets, leaves you with unforgettable memories.

Turkey isn't just a country—it's an experience, a story, and an adventure all rolled into one. It's where the past and present collide, creating a vibrant and dynamic culture that welcomes travelers with open arms. Whether you're drawn by its history, landscapes, or people, Turkey promises to leave an indelible mark on your heart.

As you prepare to explore this incredible land, remember that every corner of Turkey has a story to tell. Are you ready to listen? Let's dive into the wonders of Turkey together.

CHAPTER 1

Turkey Unveiled

Did you know that Türkiye, often referred to as the bridge between continents, is home to a staggering 85 million people?

Turkey, officially known as the Republic of Türkiye, is a fascinating country straddling two continents, with most of its landmass in Anatolia (Asia Minor) in West Asia and a smaller region, East Thrace, in Southeast Europe. This unique positioning makes it a cultural and geographical bridge between East and West.

Turkey's strategic location is highlighted by its borders with eight countries: the Black Sea lies to its north, Georgia, Armenia, Azerbaijan, and Iran are to its east, Iraq, Syria, and the Mediterranean Sea define its southern boundary, while the Aegean Sea, Greece, and Bulgaria line its western frontier.

With a population exceeding 85 million, Turkey is a tapestry of cultural diversity. While the majority are ethnic Turks, the Kurdish community represents the largest minority. Officially secular, Turkey is predominantly Muslim, a blend of modernity and tradition reflected in its cities. Ankara, the nation's capital, serves as the administrative heart, while Istanbul, a sprawling metropolis, stands as its largest city and a global hub for commerce and culture. Other notable urban centers include İzmir, Bursa, and Antalya, each adding its unique flavor to the Turkish landscape.

History of Turkey

Turkey's history is a rich tapestry that spans thousands of years, marked by the rise and fall of ancient civilizations, the spread of empires, and profound cultural transformations. Situated at the crossroads of Europe and Asia, this unique geographical position has made Turkey a cradle of human civilization, hosting some of the most significant historical events and milestones.

The history of human settlement in what is now Turkey dates back to the late Paleolithic era. Some of the world's oldest Neolithic sites, such as Gabelli Tepe, highlight Turkey's significance in early human history. Gabelli Tepe, constructed around 9600 BCE, predates iconic monuments like Stonehenge by more than 7,000 years, serving as evidence of advanced human societies in the region.

Anatolia, encompassing much of modern Turkey, played a pivotal role in the advent of agriculture. As part of the Fertile Crescent, this area witnessed early farming practices, shaping the foundation of settled human life. Significant Neolithic settlements such as Catalogue and Alaca Huyuk provide further insights into these early civilizations, showcasing their innovative lifestyles and cultural contributions.

By approximately 2000 BCE, Anatolia entered recorded history with the emergence of clay tablets from Assyrian trade colonies. Various languages like Hattian, Hurrian, Hittite, and Luwian were spoken in the region. The Hittites established a powerful kingdom centered in Hattusa, leaving behind a legacy of complex societal structures and early legal systems. Meanwhile, Troy, with its earliest layers dating to 4500 BCE, became legendary in the context of Homeric epics like the *Iliad*.

The transition to the Classical period brought profound changes as new civilizations emerged. By 750 BCE, Phrygia became a dominant power in central Anatolia, followed by the rise of cultures such as the Carians, Lycians, and Lydians. These societies reflected a resurgence of indigenous Anatolian traditions.

Greek colonization along Anatolia's western coast profoundly influenced the region. Cities such as Ephesus, Smyrna (modern İzmir), and Byzantium (later Constantinople and now Istanbul) became hubs of trade, philosophy, and science. Miletus and other cities pioneered the Ionian School of philosophy, with thinkers like Thales laying the foundations of Western rationalism.

The Persian Achaemenid Empire later absorbed much of Anatolia, leaving behind landmarks like the Temple of Artemis at Ephesus, one of the Seven Wonders of the Ancient World. Alexander the Great's conquests in the 4th century BCE heralded a period of Hellenization, blending Greek culture with local traditions.

Anatolia became an integral part of the Roman Empire following the annexation of the Kingdom of Pergamon in the 2nd century BCE. The Roman era saw significant urbanization, with cities like Ephesus boasting impressive architecture, including the Library of Celsus.

The spread of Christianity in Anatolia was catalyzed by figures like St. Paul, whose missionary journeys established some of the earliest Christian communities. By the 4th century CE, the Byzantine Empire, the eastern continuation of the Roman Empire, emerged as a dominant force. Constantinople became a cultural and religious epicenter, marked by landmarks such as the Hagia Sophia, constructed under Emperor Justinian I.

The Byzantine Empire preserved Roman traditions while fostering Greek Orthodox Christianity. Despite challenges from external invasions, it remained a major Mediterranean power until the fall of Constantinople to the Ottomans in 1453.

The arrival of Turkic peoples in Anatolia began with the Seljuk Turks in the 11th century. After their victory over the Byzantines at the Battle of Manzikert in 1071, the Seljuks established the Sultanate of Rum, marking the beginning of the Turkification of Anatolia. This period saw the integration of Turkic, Persian, and Islamic influences, profoundly shaping the region's cultural and political landscape.

The decline of the Seljuk Sultanate in the 13th century led to the rise of independent Turkish principalities, paving the way for the Ottoman Empire.

Founded in the early 14th century by Osman I, the Ottoman Empire began as a small Anatolian beylik. Under leaders like Mehmed II, who captured Constantinople in 1453, the Ottomans expanded across three continents. At its height in the 16th and 17th centuries, the empire became a dominant global power, leaving an enduring legacy in architecture, governance, and culture.

Turkey's history is a testament to its role as a bridge between civilizations. From the Neolithic settlements of Gabelli Tepe to the grandeur of the Ottoman Empire, each era has contributed to Turkey's rich and diverse heritage.

Geography

Turkey spans an area of 783,562 square kilometers (302,535 square miles). The Turkish Straits and the Sea of Marmara separate its two parts, connecting Western Asia and Southeastern Europe. Approximately 97% of Turkey's territory lies in Asia, commonly referred to as Anatolia. The eastern boundary of Anatolia is loosely defined as a line stretching from the Black Sea to the Gulf of Iskenderun.

The European portion, known as Eastern Thrace, constitutes about 3% of the land area but is home to roughly 10% of the population. Surrounded by water on three sides, Turkey borders the Aegean Sea to the west, the Black Sea to the north, and the Mediterranean Sea to the south. Land borders include Georgia, Armenia, Azerbaijan, and Iran to the east; Syria and Iraq to the south; and Greece and Bulgaria in the northwest.

Turkey is divided into seven major geographical regions: Marmara, Aegean, Central Anatolia, Black Sea, Eastern Anatolia, Southeastern Anatolia, and the Mediterranean. The central Anatolian Plateau becomes increasingly rugged as it extends eastward. Notable mountain ranges include the Köroğlu and Pontic ranges in the north and the Taurus Mountains in the south. The Lakes Region features Turkey's largest lakes, including Lake Beshear and Lake Girder.

The tectonic map of Turkey highlights various fault lines, such as the North Anatolian Fault and East Anatolian Fault. Geographers refer to the mountainous areas where the Arabian and Eurasian tectonic plates converge as the Eastern Anatolian Plateau, Iranian Plateau, or Armenian Plateau, with significant overlap between these definitions. Eastern Anatolia is home to Turkey's highest peak, Mount Ararat (5,137 meters or 16,854 feet), and its largest lake, Lake Van. This region is also the source of major rivers such as the Euphrates, Tigris, and Aras. Southeastern Anatolia encompasses the northern plains of Upper Mesopotamia.

Turkey is highly prone to earthquakes, with nearly the entire population residing in areas of seismic risk. Around 70% of the population lives in regions classified as the highest or second-highest risk zones. The Anatolian Plate is bordered by key fault systems: the North Anatolian Fault to the north, the East Anatolian Fault and Bitlis–Zagros collision zone to the east, the Hellenic and Cyprus subduction zones to the south, and the Aegean extensional zone to the west. The 1999 İzmit and Duce earthquakes highlighted the dangers of the North Anatolian Fault, now considered one of the country's most significant natural hazards. The 2023 Turkey–Syria earthquakes became the deadliest in modern Turkish history. Turkey is often unfavorably compared to Chile, which, despite a similar level of development, has a more robust earthquake preparedness system.

Climate

The coastal regions of Turkey display diverse climates based on their proximity to different seas. Areas along the Aegean and Mediterranean coasts experience a temperate Mediterranean climate, characterized by hot, dry summers and mild to cool, wet winters. The Black Sea coastal areas have a temperate oceanic climate with warm, wet summers and cool to cold, wet winters.

This region receives the highest rainfall in Turkey, with the eastern Black Sea coast averaging 2,200 millimeters (87 inches) annually, marking it as the wettest area in the country. The Marmara coast, connecting the Aegean and Black Seas, has a transitional climate, blending Mediterranean and oceanic characteristics, with warm to hot summers and cool, wet winters.

Snowfall varies significantly across regions. While snow is common in the Marmara and Black Sea coastal areas, it usually melts within days. In contrast, snowfall is rare along the Aegean coast and extremely rare along the Mediterranean coast. Winters in the Anatolian Plateau are notably harsh, with temperatures in northeastern Anatolia plunging to –30 to –40 °C (–22 to –40 °F) and snow covering the ground for up to 120 days annually. On the summits of the highest mountains, snow can persist year-round.

In central Anatolia, temperatures may fall below –20 °C (–4 °F), with the surrounding mountains being even colder. The mountain ranges near the coasts block Mediterranean influences from reaching the interior, giving the central Anatolian Plateau a continental climate with distinct seasonal contrasts.

Turkey faces significant vulnerability to climate change due to a combination of socioeconomic, climatic, and geographic factors. The country is affected in nine out of ten dimensions of climate vulnerability, such as "average annual risk to wellbeing," compared to an OECD median of two out of ten. To reduce this vulnerability, Turkey emphasizes the need for inclusive and accelerated economic growth.

The nation has committed to achieving net zero emissions by 2053, a goal requiring substantial investments but offering notable benefits, including reduced reliance on fuel imports and improved public health from lower air pollution levels.

Language and Communication Tips

Understanding the nuances of language and communication can significantly enhance your experience in Turkey, whether you're visiting for leisure, business, or cultural exploration. Turkish is the official language, spoken by the vast majority of the population. While English is widely understood in major cities, tourist hubs, and among younger generations, learning a few basic Turkish phrases can go a long way in fostering goodwill and demonstrating respect for local culture. Simple expressions like *Marhaba* (hello), *tasker Ede rim* (thank you), and *lateen* (please) are often appreciated and can help break the ice in casual interactions.

When communicating with locals, it's important to note that Turkish culture values politeness and hospitality. People are generally warm and willing to assist, even if there's a language barrier. Gestures, facial expressions, and patience play an integral role in bridging communication gaps. If you're unsure of how to convey your message, using a combination of simple English words, hand gestures, or a translation app can be highly effective. Many Turks enjoy engaging with visitors and may go out of their way to help you, especially in less touristy areas.

Non-verbal communication also carries significant weight in Turkey. For instance, maintaining eye contact shows sincerity and interest, while a firm but not overly strong handshake is a common form of greeting. A slight nod or bow of the head conveys respect. When addressing someone formally, it's customary to use titles such as *Bey* (Mr.) or *Hanmi* (Ms.) following their first name, as a sign of respect. This practice is particularly prevalent in business or formal settings.

Humor and light-hearted conversations are well-received, but it's wise to avoid discussing sensitive topics like politics or religion unless you know the person well. Turkish people often enjoy talking about their culture, history, and cuisine, which can provide excellent opportunities to bond and learn more about the country. Asking questions about Turkish traditions or sharing your experiences with Turkish food can lead to enriching conversations.

While exploring smaller towns or rural areas, you may encounter fewer English speakers. In such cases, having a pocket dictionary or downloading a language app can be extremely helpful. Turkish is a phonetic language, meaning words are pronounced as they are written, making it relatively easy to pick up basic phrases. Locals often appreciate even modest attempts to speak their language and may respond more openly to those who make the effort.

Lastly, when it comes to communication etiquette, remember that Turks value hospitality and personal relationships. In social settings, you might be invited for tea or coffee as a gesture of friendliness. Accepting such invitations when possible is not only polite but can also deepen your understanding of Turkish culture. Whether in casual or professional settings, showing warmth, patience, and an eagerness to connect will ensure positive interactions during your time in Turkey.

Religion and Cultural Etiquette

Turkey is a secular state, ensuring freedom of religion and conscience through its constitution. The majority of the population identifies as Muslim, primarily Sunni, making up approximately 99% of the population. Alevi Muslims form a significant minority, with estimates of their proportion varying widely.

Non-Muslim communities, while a smaller percentage of the population today, include Armenians, Assyrians, Greek Orthodox Christians, Catholics, Chaldeans, Protestants, and Jews. Historically, these communities played a vital role in the cultural and religious diversity of the region. Presently, Turkey is home to around 439 churches and synagogues, reflecting the continued presence of its Christian and Jewish populations.

The religious landscape of Turkey has evolved significantly over the past century. While non-Muslims constituted nearly 19% of the population in 1914, their numbers have declined over time. Today, non-Muslims account for less than 1% of the population. Despite this, Turkey has the largest Jewish community among Muslim-majority countries, further highlighting its historical role as a melting pot of faiths.

Overall, Turkey's religious framework reflects a balance between its secular governance and the predominantly Muslim beliefs of its population, alongside its commitment to preserving the rights and traditions of its diverse religious minorities.

Festivals and Celebrations

Turkey is a country with a rich and diverse cultural heritage, and its festivals and celebrations reflect the country's unique blend of traditions, religious observances, and historical influences. These events offer a fascinating glimpse into Turkish culture, where festivals are marked by lively celebrations, music, dance, food, and community gatherings. Below are some of the most important and widely celebrated festivals in Turkey, showcasing the country's vibrant traditions.

Religious Holidays

➤ Ramazan Bayram (Eid al-Fitr)

Ramazan Bayram, or Eid al-Fitr, is one of the most significant religious holidays in Turkey, marking the end of Ramadan, the Islamic holy month of fasting. The holiday is a time for family reunions, feasts, and giving to those in need. In Turkey, people dress in their finest clothes, visit friends and family, and visit the graves of loved ones. The streets are filled with joy, and special sweets like *baklava* and *gulag* are prepared and shared. Many Turks also attend mosque for special prayers.

➤ Kurban Bayram (Eid al-Adha)

Kurban Bayram, or Eid al-Adha, is another major religious holiday in Turkey, commemorating the willingness of the Prophet Ibrahim to sacrifice his son Ismail as an act of obedience to God. In Turkey, families typically sacrifice an animal (usually a sheep, cow, or goat) and distribute the meat to the poor, friends, and family. The holiday is marked by prayers at the mosque and gatherings with loved ones. This festival is celebrated with a deep sense of community and charity.

➤ Mevlid Kandola (Birth of the Prophet Muhammad)

Mevlid Kandola is the celebration of the birth of the Prophet Muhammad, observed by many Turkish Muslims, particularly in the form of prayers and religious gatherings. On this night, mosques hold special prayers, and people gather to listen to religious lectures and read passages from the Quran. Many communities also serve food and distribute sweets.

National Festivals

➤ Republic Day (Cumhuriyet Bayram)

Republic Day, celebrated on October 29th, marks the founding of the Turkish Republic in 1923 by Mustafa Kemal Atatürk. This national holiday is celebrated with ceremonies, parades, and fireworks throughout Turkey. In the capital, Ankara, there are grand celebrations, including a military parade and a speech by the president. People often display the Turkish flag, and many participate in patriotic events to honor the nation's history.

➤ National Sovereignty and Children's Day (Uluas Gemelli vet Cockup Bayram)

Held on April 23rd, this unique holiday celebrates both the sovereignty of the Turkish Grand National Assembly and honors children. The holiday is especially significant as it's the only national holiday dedicated specifically to children. Schools and communities across Turkey host special events, including performances, plays, and parades, with children playing a central role. In addition, the Turkish president often invites children from different countries to participate in the celebrations, promoting international friendship and understanding.

➤ Victory Day (Zafer Bajrami)

Victory Day is celebrated on August 30th in Turkey to commemorate the victory of the Turkish forces in the Battle of Dubliner, a turning point in the Turkish War of Independence. It is a patriotic holiday marked by parades, particularly in the capital, Ankara, and other major cities. People gather to honor the soldiers who fought for Turkey's independence, and many participate in ceremonies at monuments and military memorials.

Traditional and Cultural Festivals

➤ Hydrillas Festival

Hydrillas is a vibrant celebration that takes place on May 6th, marking the arrival of spring. It is rooted in Turkic and Islamic traditions, symbolizing renewal and the blessings of nature. People celebrate with open-air parties, dancing, singing, and feasting. In some regions, people jump over bonfires to purify themselves and bring good luck. This festival is especially popular in the Aegean and Marmara regions, where locals engage in fun activities like fortune-telling, picnics, and street parades.

➤ International Istanbul Film Festival

The International Istanbul Film Festival, held annually in April, is one of the most prestigious cultural events in Turkey. The festival attracts filmmakers and film lovers from all over the world, showcasing both international and Turkish cinema. Screenings are held in various venues throughout Istanbul, and the event includes awards, panel discussions, and parties. It has become a major part of Istanbul's cultural scene and a must-attend event for film enthusiasts.

➤ Aspen Dos Opera and Ballet Festival

Held in the ancient city of Aspen Dos, near Antalya, the Aspen Dos Opera and Ballet Festival is a grand cultural event that takes place every summer. It is held in the ancient Aspen Dos Theater, one of the best-preserved Roman theaters in the world, and features performances by world-renowned opera singers, ballet dancers, and orchestras. The combination of stunning performances and the incredible acoustics of the ancient theater makes this festival a memorable experience for all attendees.

Selçuk Efes Artemis Festival

This festival, held in the ancient city of Ephesus in Selçuk, celebrates the heritage of the ancient city and its famed Temple of Artemis, one of the Seven Wonders of the Ancient World. The festival typically features traditional music, dance performances, and historical reenactments, allowing visitors to experience the rich cultural and historical significance of the region. It's a perfect way to explore Turkey's deep connection to its ancient civilizations.

Regional Festivals

➤ Kyeis Dragon Boat Festival

Held annually in the village of Kyeis, located in southwestern Turkey, the Kyeis Dragon Boat Festival is a lively and colorful event that celebrates Turkish folk traditions. The festival features dragon boat races, where teams row elaborately decorated boats, as well as music, dancing, and local food. It's a great way to experience the culture and spirit of the Turkish Mediterranean coast.

➤ Cappadocia Balloon Festival

One of the most famous and unique festivals in Turkey, the Cappadocia Balloon Festival takes place every July in the stunning region of Cappadocia, known for its fairy chimneys and hot air balloon rides. During the festival, hundreds of colorful balloons fill the sky, creating a breathtaking scene. The event includes not only balloon rides but also music performances, light shows, and cultural activities that attract visitors from all over the world.

Festivals and celebrations in Turkey offer a wonderful opportunity to explore the country's rich cultural heritage, its deep-rooted traditions, and its vibrant, diverse communities. From religious holidays like Ramadan Bayramı and Kurban Bayramı to national events such as Republic Day and cultural festivals like the Hydrillas Festival, Turkey is a country that celebrates its past and present with enthusiasm and pride. Whether you are visiting for a religious holiday, a cultural event, or simply to immerse yourself in the local traditions, you will find that Turkey's festivals are an essential part of its national identity and provide lasting memories for those who partake in them.

Top Reasons to Visit

Turkey, a country that bridges Europe and Asia, is a land of mesmerizing landscapes, rich history, vibrant culture, and mouthwatering cuisine. Whether you're a history enthusiast, a nature lover, or someone seeking an adventurous escape, Turkey offers something for everyone. Here are the top reasons why you should consider visiting Turkey for your next vacation:

➤ Rich History and Ancient Ruins

Turkey is home to some of the world's most iconic ancient ruins, making it a must-visit destination for history buffs. From the legendary city of Troy, immortalized by Homer's Iliad, to the spectacular Roman ruins at Ephesus, Turkey is a treasure trove of historical sites. The ancient city of Petra and the Temple of

Artemis, one of the Seven Wonders of the Ancient World, offer an unparalleled look into ancient civilizations. Don't miss the surreal ruins of Persepolis, or the fascinating rock-hewn churches of Cappadocia.

➢ Breathtaking Landscapes

Turkey boasts some of the most diverse and breathtaking landscapes in the world. You can explore the rocky fairy chimneys and unique volcanic formations of Cappadocia, go hiking along the stunning Lycian Way with views of the Mediterranean Sea, or unwind on the golden beaches of the Aegean and Mediterranean coasts. The country is also home to the striking white travertine terraces of Pamuk kale, where hot spring water creates terraces of mineral-rich pools, perfect for a natural spa experience. Whether you prefer the mountains, beaches, or rolling hills, Turkey's scenery will leave you in awe.

➢ Delicious Cuisine

Turkish cuisine is renowned for its variety, flavors, and fresh ingredients. From savory dishes like kebabs and mezes to sweet treats such as baklava and Turkish delight, food lovers will find their hearts (and stomachs) content in Turkey. Don't forget to try traditional dishes like manta (Turkish dumplings), pied (Turkish pizza), and kofta (meatballs). Pair these delicious meals with a glass of rake, the country's famous aniseed-flavored spirit, or a cup of Turkish tea, which is integral to Turkish culture.

➢ Cultural Heritage and Traditions

Turkey's cultural heritage is a blend of Eastern and Western influences, combining elements from the ancient Greek, Roman, Byzantine, and Ottoman civilizations. The country has a long history of art, architecture, and literature, which you can experience through its ancient mosques, churches, palaces, and museums. Istanbul, the only city in the world that spans two continents, is a vibrant metropolis that showcases the diverse cultural influences that have shaped Turkey. The stunning Hagia Sophia, the Blue Mosque, and Tokai Palace are just a few examples of Turkey's wealth of cultural landmarks.

➤ Stunning Beaches and Resort Towns

Turkey is famous for its spectacular coastline, which stretches along the Aegean and Mediterranean Seas. The coastal towns of Bodrum, Fisheye, and Antalya are popular beach destinations where you can relax on sandy beaches, enjoy water sports, or take boat trips along the turquoise waters. The southern coast, known as the Turkish Riviera, boasts luxury resorts and charming seaside villages. Whether you prefer lively resorts or quieter, secluded beaches, Turkey's coastline offers plenty of opportunities for sun, sea, and relaxation.

➤ Warm Hospitality

One of the most memorable aspects of visiting Turkey is the warmth and generosity of the Turkish people. Turkish hospitality is world-renowned, and visitors are often treated like family. It's common for locals to offer tea, share stories, and extend a warm welcome to tourists. Whether you're exploring a bustling market in Istanbul or visiting a small village, you'll quickly realize that the people of Turkey take great pride in sharing their culture and making visitors feel at home.

➤ Unique Architecture

Turkey is home to some of the world's most extraordinary architectural feats. From the Byzantine mosaics in Istanbul's Hagia Sophia to the Ottoman-era palaces, mosques, and bridges, Turkey's buildings reflect a rich blend of architectural styles. The elegant mosques of Istanbul and the intricate tile work of the Salmiya Mosque in Edirne are a testament to the country's diverse architectural legacy. In addition, the ancient rock-hewn dwellings in Cappadocia and the underground cities carved into the region's soft volcanic rock are unique examples of human ingenuity and adaptation to the environment.

➤ Vibrant Markets and Bazaars

No visit to Turkey is complete without exploring its colorful markets and bazaars. The Grand Bazaar in Istanbul is one of the largest and oldest covered markets in the world, offering an eclectic mix of jewelry, textiles, spices, and handcrafted goods. Whether you're searching for traditional Turkish carpets, handmade ceramics, or local spices like saffron and sumac, the markets of Turkey offer an authentic shopping experience. The spice bazaars, particularly in Istanbul, are a sensory delight, with an array of smells and colors that will transport you to another world.

➤ Adventure and Outdoor Activities

For those seeking adventure, Turkey offers plenty of opportunities for outdoor activities. Cappadocia is famous for its hot air balloon rides, offering stunning aerial views of the fairy chimneys and unique rock formations. You can go hiking in the lush forests of the Black Sea region, paragliding over the stunning Loudened Beach, or even white-water rafting in the Köprülü Canyon. The varied landscapes, including mountains, forests, and coastlines, provide an ideal setting for adventure sports and nature lovers alike.

➤ Affordable Travel

Turkey offers great value for money, especially when compared to many Western European destinations. Accommodations range from luxurious five-star resorts to affordable guesthouses and boutique hotels. The cost of dining and transportation is relatively low, and you can enjoy an authentic experience without breaking the bank. This affordability makes Turkey an attractive option for travelers looking to experience rich culture, history, and natural beauty without overspending.

Turkey is a captivating country with a blend of history, culture, natural beauty, and hospitality that makes it a unique destination for travelers. Whether you're drawn to the ancient ruins, stunning landscapes, vibrant bazaars, or delectable food, Turkey offers an unforgettable experience for every kind of traveler. With its rich cultural heritage, diverse attractions, and warm, welcoming people, Turkey is a destination that will leave you with lasting memories.

........And Then Your Adventure Begins........

TURKEY TRAVEL GUIDE

CHAPTER 2

Planning Your Trip to Turkey

Did you know that Turkey is one of the few countries in the world where you can literally walk through two continents?

S panning both Europe and Asia, Turkey offers travelers a unique opportunity to experience the blending of different cultures, histories, and landscapes. Whether you're drawn to the bustling streets of Istanbul, the tranquil beaches of the Mediterranean, or the ancient ruins that dot the landscape, Turkey is a destination that caters to all types of travelers.

Planning your trip to Turkey may feel like a daunting task, but with the right knowledge and preparation, it can be an exciting and enriching experience. From determining the best time to visit to choosing the ideal destinations, there are a multitude of factors to consider. Whether it's your first time in Turkey or you're returning to explore more of its hidden gems, this chapter will provide you with all the essential tips and information to ensure your trip is seamless, unforgettable, and tailored to your interests. Let's begin with the most important step: preparing for your Turkish adventure.

Best Time to Explore Turkey

Turkey's diverse landscape and rich culture make it a year-round destination, but the best time to visit depends largely on what you want to experience. Whether you're looking to explore ancient ruins, enjoy the Mediterranean beaches, or hike through scenic landscapes, the timing of your trip can significantly enhance your experience.

➤ Spring (March to May)

Spring is often regarded as one of the best times to visit Turkey, especially if you prefer milder weather and fewer crowds. The temperatures in major cities like Istanbul and Ankara are comfortable, ranging from 10°C (50°F) to 20°C (68°F), making it ideal for sightseeing and outdoor activities. This season is also perfect for nature lovers, as the landscapes come alive with blooming flowers, lush greenery, and colorful gardens.

In the coastal regions like the Aegean and Mediterranean coasts, the weather is warm enough to enjoy outdoor activities without the summer heat. Spring is also the perfect time to visit historical sites like Ephesus, Troy, and the ancient cities of the Lycian Coast, as the crowds are still manageable.

➤ Summer (June to August)

Summer in Turkey can be hot, especially in the inland regions like Central Anatolia and Eastern Anatolia, where temperatures often soar above 35°C (95°F). However, if you're planning to visit the coastal areas, this is the time to soak up the sun and enjoy the beaches. The Mediterranean and Aegean coasts experience the perfect beach weather, with temperatures averaging around 28°C (82°F) to 35°C (95°F).

Summer is also the peak tourist season, especially in popular cities like Istanbul, Antalya, and Bodrum. This means there will be larger crowds, higher prices, and longer lines at major attractions. However, it's also when many cultural festivals and events take place, offering a chance to experience Turkey's vibrant music, art, and culinary scenes. Just be prepared for higher accommodation costs and busy tourist spots.

➤ Fall (September to November)

Fall is another fantastic time to visit Turkey, especially for those who prefer comfortable temperatures and a more relaxed atmosphere. The weather in cities like Istanbul, Cappadocia, and the Aegean coast is pleasant, with temperatures ranging from 15°C (59°F) to 25°C (77°F), making it ideal for exploring the historical sites, enjoying outdoor activities, and taking in the breathtaking landscapes.

This season also brings the harvest time in Turkey, making it perfect for food enthusiasts who want to experience local cuisine at its finest. In addition, fall is a great time for hot air ballooning in Cappadocia, as the skies are clear, and the weather is still mild. It's also the time for many festivals and cultural events, including wine festivals in the Aegean region and harvest festivals across the country.

➢ Winter (December to February)

Winter in Turkey brings a completely different charm to the country. While the coastal regions remain mild, with temperatures ranging from 10°C (50°F) to 15°C (59°F), the inland and mountainous areas, especially in places like Cappadocia and the eastern part of the country, experience snow and freezing temperatures. This is a great time to explore Turkey's winter sports resorts like Uludağ, Erinyes, and Palankeen, where skiing and snowboarding are popular.

If you're interested in a quieter, off-the-beaten-path experience, winter is an excellent time to visit the country's major attractions. The ancient ruins, such as those in Ephesus and Pamuk kale, are much less crowded, allowing you to fully immerse yourself in the historical significance without the hustle and bustle of peak season tourists.

For those seeking a cultural experience, Istanbul in winter is magical, with its cozy cafes and fewer crowds. You can also enjoy

Turkey's hot springs and spa resorts in places like Pamuk kale and Yalova, which are particularly inviting during the colder months.

Ultimately, the best time to visit Turkey depends on your preferences. Spring and fall offer the most comfortable weather for sightseeing and outdoor activities, while summer is ideal for beach lovers, despite the crowds and heat. Winter is perfect for those looking to experience Turkey's snowy landscapes or indulge in winter sports. No matter when you decide to visit, Turkey's rich history, diverse landscapes, and warm hospitality ensure that it will be an unforgettable experience.

Essential Items to Pack

When planning a trip to Turkey, packing efficiently is key to making sure you have everything you need to enjoy your visit comfortably. Turkey's diverse geography, culture, and climate mean you'll need to consider various factors while packing, from the weather conditions to the activities you'll be participating in. Here's a list of essential items to ensure you're well-prepared for your trip.

➢ Appropriate Clothing for Varying Climates

Turkey's weather can vary greatly depending on the region and the time of year. For instance, the coastal regions can be hot and sunny during summer, while the inland areas experience extreme temperatures, especially in winter. Be sure to pack clothing for all seasons.

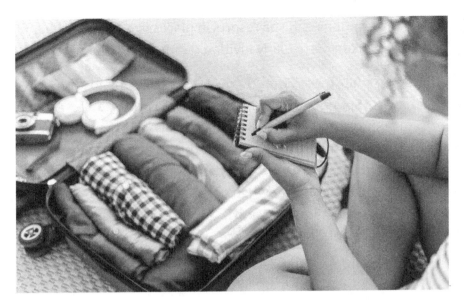

- **Summer**: Light, breathable fabrics like cotton and linen are perfect for warm days, especially in the coastal areas and during the warmer months. Don't forget your sunglasses, sun hat, and sunscreen for protection against the sun.
- **Winter**: If you're visiting during the winter months or traveling to higher altitudes, like in Cappadocia or Eastern Anatolia, a warm coat, gloves, and layered clothing will be essential.
- **For All Seasons**: Pack comfortable shoes for walking, especially if you plan to explore historical sites or walk around cobbled streets in cities like Istanbul. A lightweight scarf or shawl is also useful for both practical and cultural reasons.

➢ Power Adapter and Voltage Converter

Turkey uses the **Type C** and **Type Of** power outlets with a standard voltage of **220V** and a frequency of **50Hz**. If your devices have a different plug type, bring a universal travel adapter. A voltage converter may also be necessary if your devices don't support the 220V power supply.

➢ Comfortable Footwear

Turkey is a country filled with historical sites, mountains, and coastal areas to explore, so comfortable walking shoes are a must. Whether you're hiking through Cappadocia or strolling through ancient ruins like Ephesus, sturdy shoes will make your journey much more enjoyable. If you're heading to the beach or visiting hot springs, flip-flops or sandals are also recommended.

➢ Sunscreen and Sunglasses

The sun can be quite strong, especially along the Mediterranean and Aegean coasts during summer. Pack a high-SPF sunscreen to protect your skin from harmful UV rays, and make sure to bring sunglasses to shield your eyes from the glare. A hat or cap can also provide extra protection from the sun.

➢ Swimwear

If you're planning to visit the Turkish coast, beaches, or resorts, pack swimwear for a swim in the Mediterranean, Aegean, or Black Sea. Popular beach destinations like Antalya, Bodrum, and Fisheye will likely have pools and seaside activities.

➢ Camera or Smartphone

Turkey is home to some of the world's most breathtaking landscapes and historical landmarks, so don't forget a camera or smartphone to capture your memories. If you're visiting places like Pamuk kale's white terraces, the ancient ruins of Ephesus, or the surreal landscapes of Cappadocia, you'll want to take plenty of photos. Be sure to bring extra memory cards and a portable charger.

➢ Travel Guidebook or Map

While smartphones and digital navigation apps like Google Maps are handy, having a physical map or guidebook can be useful, especially when traveling to more remote areas with limited internet access. You can also learn more about Turkey's history, culture, and hidden gems by reading a guidebook along the way.

➢ Medication and Health Supplies

Traveling to a new country often means exposure to new allergens or health challenges. Make sure to bring any prescription medications you may need, along with a small first-aid kit containing items like pain relievers, band-aids, antiseptic wipes, and insect repellent. If you wear glasses or contact lenses, bring a spare pair, as well as any lens solution you might need.

➢ Travel Documents

Ensure you have all your important travel documents ready and in a safe place. These include:

- **Passport**: Ensure your passport is valid for at least six months beyond your planned stay in Turkey.
- **Visa**: Depending on your nationality, you may need a visa to enter Turkey. You can apply for an e-Visa online or at a Turkish consulate before your trip.
- **Travel Insurance**: It's always a good idea to have travel insurance in case of unexpected events like medical emergencies, cancellations, or lost luggage.

➢ Money and Credit Cards

The currency in Turkey is the **Turkish Lira (TRY),** and while major credit cards are widely accepted in tourist areas, it's a good idea to carry some cash, especially when visiting smaller towns, local markets, or rural areas. ATMs are readily available, but be mindful of any foreign transaction fees charged by your bank. Always keep your money in a secure place, like a money belt or lockable bag.

➢ Reusable Water Bottle

Tap water in Turkey is generally safe to drink, but it's always a good idea to double-check in rural areas or small towns. A reusable water bottle is a convenient way to stay hydrated while reducing plastic waste. Many public places also have water fountains where you can refill your bottle.

➢ A Turkish Phrasebook or Translation App

While many people in Turkey speak some level of English, especially in tourist areas, it's still helpful to learn a few basic Turkish phrases. Carrying a pocket-sized phrasebook or using a translation app can help you navigate day-to-day interactions and make your trip more enjoyable. Simple phrases like "Marhaba" (Hello), "Tasker Ede rim" (Thank you), and "Lateen" (Please) can go a long way in showing respect for the local culture.

➤ Cultural and Religious Respect Items

Turkey is a country with rich cultural and religious diversity. When visiting religious sites, such as mosques or churches, make sure to dress modestly. Women may be asked to cover their heads, so a lightweight scarf is recommended. When visiting mosques, both men and women are typically required to remove their shoes before entering.

➤ Small Backpack or Daypack

A small backpack or daypack is ideal for carrying essentials like water, sunscreen, snacks, a camera, and any other small items you need for a day of exploring. It's much more comfortable than lugging around a heavy suitcase while touring ancient sites or hiking through scenic landscapes.

Packing for a trip to Turkey requires some careful thought due to the country's varied climates and activities. By bringing along these essentials, you'll be well-prepared for everything from city tours and historical explorations to beach getaways and cultural experiences. A little bit of planning ahead will ensure your Turkish adventure is smooth, enjoyable, and unforgettable.

Visa and Insurance Requirements for Turkey

Visa Requirements for Turkey

Turkey's visa policy varies depending on the nationality of the traveler. Here's an overview of what you need to know about Turkey's visa requirements.

> ➢ **Visa-Free Entry**

Citizens from some countries do not require a visa to enter Turkey for short stays, typically for tourism or business purposes. These countries include, but are not limited to:

- **European Union (EU)** member states
- **United States**

- **Canada**
- **Australia**
- **New Zealand**
- **Japan**
- **South Korea**

Citizens from these countries can stay in Turkey for up to 90 days within a 180-day period without the need for a visa. However, this visa-free stay is limited to tourism, business, or transit purposes. Be sure to check the specific rules for your country, as some nations may have slightly different requirements or limits.

➤ e-Visa (Electronic Visa)

Many nationalities that are not eligible for visa-free entry can apply for an **e-Visa** to enter Turkey. The e-Visa is an online application process that allows travelers to apply for a tourist or business visa before arriving in Turkey.

The e-Visa is typically valid for **90 days** and allows **multiple entries**. The application is simple and can be completed on the Turkish Ministry of Foreign Affairs website. You will need to provide personal information, travel details, and passport details. Once approved, you will receive the e-Visa via email, which you must print and present upon arrival in Turkey.

➤ Sticker Visa (At a Consulate)

Travelers from countries that are not eligible for the e-Visa can obtain a **sticker visa** by applying at a Turkish consulate or embassy in their home country or in a neighboring country. The visa application process may require submitting documents such as:

- Valid passport with at least six months of validity beyond your planned stay.
- Proof of sufficient funds to cover your stay in Turkey.
- A confirmed return ticket.
- A visa application form.
- Passport-sized photos.

The processing time for a sticker visa can take several days to weeks, depending on the consulate.

Insurance Requirements for Turkey

While Turkey does not legally require tourists to have travel insurance for entry, having adequate travel insurance is highly recommended. Travel insurance can protect you from unexpected events, such as medical emergencies, flight cancellations, lost luggage, or other unforeseen circumstances.

➤ Medical Insurance

If you're visiting Turkey, medical insurance is one of the most important types of coverage you should consider. While Turkish hospitals are modern and well-equipped, healthcare can be expensive for foreign visitors. If you require emergency medical care or need to visit a doctor, having medical insurance will provide peace of mind and ensure that your treatment costs are covered.

Some key points to consider about travel medical insurance for Turkey:

- **Emergency Medical Expenses**: Covers treatment in case of accidents or illness.
- **Medical Evacuation**: In case you need to be transported to a better facility or back home due to medical reasons.
- **Repatriation of Remains**: In unfortunate cases of death, this covers the cost of returning remains to your home country.
- **Pre-existing Conditions**: Be sure to check whether your medical insurance covers any pre-existing conditions, as some policies may not.

➤ Trip Cancellation and Interruption Insurance

Trip cancellation insurance covers the costs of canceled flights or accommodation if something unexpected arises, like a family emergency, illness, or flight cancellations. This can be especially useful if you've made non-refundable reservations or invested a significant amount in your trip.

Several international travel insurance providers offer coverage for travelers visiting Turkey. Some of the well-known companies include:

- World Nomads
- Allianz Global Assistance
- Travel Guard
- AXA Travel Insurance

Many Turkish travel agencies and tour operators also offer insurance as part of their travel packages, so check if you can get insurance through them as well.

➢ Tourist Health Insurance in Turkey

If you're traveling as part of an organized tour, some tour operators may offer **Turkish tourist health insurance** as part of their package. This insurance is specifically designed for foreign tourists and covers basic medical care, including emergency medical expenses.

EU Citizens and Turkish Health Insurance If you are a citizen of the European Union (EU), you are eligible for emergency medical care in Turkey through the European Health Insurance Card (EHIC). However, the EHIC doesn't cover all medical expenses, and you may need to pay upfront for some services and claim reimbursement. It's still recommended to have additional travel insurance to cover all possible health-related incidents.

Finally

- **Check Requirements**: Before traveling to Turkey, make sure to check the latest visa and insurance requirements for your nationality, as these can change.
- **Ensure Adequate Coverage**: Make sure your travel insurance provides adequate medical coverage and covers unexpected trip interruptions or cancellations.
- **Travel Insurance for Adventure Activities**: If you plan to engage in adventurous activities like hiking, diving, or hot

air ballooning (popular in Cappadocia), ensure that your insurance covers these activities.

By ensuring that you have the correct visa and adequate insurance, you can enjoy a worry-free and smooth trip to Turkey.

Transportation Options to Turkey

Turkey is a significant travel hub, well-connected to the rest of the world by air, land, and sea. The country's strategic location at the crossroads of Europe and Asia makes it accessible from numerous global destinations. Here's a detailed guide to the various transportation options to Turkey, including air, land, and water routes.

Air Travel: Flying to Turkey

Turkey's air transport network is one of the most developed in the world, with several major international airports and numerous flight connections to cities across the globe.

> ## Major Airports in Turkey

- **Istanbul Airport (IST):** Located on the European side of Istanbul, this is the largest and busiest airport in Turkey, serving as a major international hub with flights to destinations worldwide. It is the primary airport for international flights to Turkey.

- **Sabiha Gökçen International Airport (SAW)**: Also in Istanbul, this airport primarily handles low-cost carriers and flights to Europe, the Middle East, and some regional destinations.

- **Antalya Airport (AYT)**: Located in the southern part of Turkey, Antalya is one of the most popular destinations for tourists traveling to the Mediterranean coast, especially during the summer months.
- **Ankara Sambora Airport (ESB)**: Serving the capital city, Ankara, this airport is the gateway for travelers heading to central Turkey.
- **Izmir Adnan Menderes Airport (ADB)**: Located on the Aegean coast, Izmir's airport is well connected to European cities and serves as a gateway to the western parts of Turkey.

> ### Flights from Different Countries

- **From the United States**: There are direct flights from major US cities like New York (JFK), Los Angeles (LAX), and Chicago (ORD) to Istanbul, with airlines such as Turkish Airlines, American Airlines, and Delta.
- **From Europe**: Istanbul is very well connected to major European cities like London, Paris, Berlin, and Rome, with multiple daily flights. Turkish Airlines offers direct flights to Istanbul from almost all European capitals.
- **From the Middle East**: Countries in the Middle East, including the United Arab Emirates, Saudi Arabia, Qatar, and Jordan, have frequent flights to Turkey, with both regional airlines like Emirates and Qatar Airways, and Turkish Airlines offering services.
- **From Asia**: Turkey has direct flights from several Asian countries, including China, India, Japan, and South Korea, with Turkish Airlines, China Eastern Airlines, and Korean Air providing options.
- **From Africa**: Direct flights from cities such as Cairo (Egypt), Cape Town (South Africa), and Nairobi (Kenya) are available via airlines like EgyptAir and Turkish Airlines.

Land Travel: Reaching Turkey by Road and Rail

Turkey shares land borders with Greece, Bulgaria, Georgia, Armenia, Azerbaijan (Nakhichevan exclave), Iran, Iraq, and Syria, and traveling by land is possible from many countries in these regions.

➢ From Europe

- **Buses**: There are numerous international bus services operating from Europe to Turkey. Major departure cities include Vienna, Budapest, Athens, Sofia, and Belgrade, with buses traveling directly to Istanbul or other major cities. The bus journey can take from 12 hours to over 24 hours, depending on the departure city.
- **Driving**: If you are driving from Europe, the most common route is through Bulgaria and Greece into Turkey. From Sofia or Athens, you can drive to Istanbul, which typically takes 7-10 hours, depending on traffic and border crossing times.

➢ From the Middle East and Asia

- **From Iran**: There are bus services from Tehran and other Iranian cities to Istanbul and Van, with travel times ranging from 24 to 36 hours, depending on the route and stops. Travelers can also cross by car through the Bazargan border gate.
- **From Armenia**: Travel by bus or car from Yerevan to Istanbul or Van is possible, but border crossings may be subject to restrictions or delays due to political reasons. A more common route is via Tbilisi, Georgia.
- **From Iraq**: Bus services from Baghdad and Erbil to Turkey are available, typically reaching Istanbul or Diyarbakir. It's important to note that security conditions in border regions can affect travel routes.

➢ From Central Asia

For travelers coming from Kazakhstan, Uzbekistan, or Kyrgyzstan, long-distance trains or buses can take you to Turkey, but the journey is lengthy and may involve multiple transfers. Many travelers opt for a flight to Istanbul due to the vast distance and long travel times by land.

➢ Trains

International train services operate between Turkey and some neighboring countries. The Trans-Balkan Express connects Sofia (Bulgaria) to Istanbul. Another notable train is the Bosphorus Express that links Istanbul with Bucharest (Romania). Train services, though, are less frequent than buses and may take longer, so passengers often opt for quicker options like flights or buses.

Sea Travel: Reaching Turkey by Sea

Turkey is surrounded by seas on three sides—the Aegean Sea to the west, the Mediterranean Sea to the south, and the Black Sea to the north. Several international sea routes serve Turkey's ports, providing options for cruise ships, ferries, and cargo vessels.

➢ From Europe

Ferries: Ferry services are available between several European countries and Turkey, including Italy, Greece, and Cyprus. For example, ferries from Venice or Ancona (Italy) travel to Istanbul or Esme, while Piraeus (Athens) is a major departure point for ferries traveling to İstanbul, Kanadas, Bodrum, and Cosme.

Cruise Ships: Many Mediterranean cruises stop at Turkish ports like Istanbul, Kusanagi, Bodrum, and Antalya. Some cruises operate in the Black Sea region, stopping at ports such as Trabzon and Sinope.

➢ From the Middle East

Ferries and Cruise Ships: Ferries and cruise ships from cities like Beirut (Lebanon), Alexandria (Egypt), and Haifa (Israel) often travel to Istanbul or southern Turkish ports. However, ferry services may be limited depending on geopolitical conditions and the season.

➢ From North Africa

Ferries: There are also ferry routes from Tunis (Tunisia) and Algiers (Algeria) to Turkey, but these services are not as frequent. Cruises along the Mediterranean may also include Turkish ports.

➢ From Russia and Ukraine

Ferries and cruise ships from Odessa (Ukraine) and Sochi (Russia) often stop at Trabzon, Sinope, and Istanbul. However, these routes may not operate year-round, and their availability depends on the political and weather conditions in the region.

Whether you prefer to travel by air, sea, or land, Turkey offers multiple options for reaching the country from virtually every continent. Air travel is the most common and efficient method, but land and sea routes are also viable alternatives for travelers coming from neighboring regions or those seeking a more adventurous approach to their journey.

CHAPTER 3

ISTANBUL

Did you know that Turkey welcomed over 51 million tourists in 2022, making it one of the world's top travel destinations?

This incredible influx of visitors has led to a diverse range of accommodations to suit every traveler's budget and preferences. From luxurious seaside resorts along the turquoise coasts to charming boutique hotels nestled in historic towns, Turkey offers an impressive array of lodging options.

Istanbul, the largest city in Turkey, spans the Bosporus Strait, serving as a bridge between Europe and Asia. Known as the country's economic, cultural, and historic capital, Istanbul is home to over 15 million residents, representing 19% of Turkey's population. It is the most populous city in Europe and ranks as the sixteenth-largest city in the world.

Originally established as Byzantium in the 7th century BCE by Greek settlers from Megara, the city underwent a transformative history. In 330 CE, Roman Emperor Constantine the Great made it his imperial capital, naming it New Rome before renaming it Constantinople in his honor. By 1930, the city officially adopted its modern name, Istanbul, derived from the Greek phrase *Eis tan Polin* ("to the city"), a colloquial reference used since the 11th century.

Istanbul served as an imperial capital for nearly 1,600 years, holding prominence under the Byzantine (330–1204), Latin (1204–1261), late Byzantine (1261–1453), and Ottoman (1453–1922) empires. Throughout history, it grew as a key hub along the Silk Road and became one of the most significant cities in the world. During the Roman and Byzantine periods, it played a central role in advancing Christianity, hosting four of the first seven ecumenical councils. After the Fall of Constantinople in 1453, it became an Islamic stronghold and later the seat of the Ottoman Caliphate in 1517. Following the Turkish War of Independence in 1923, Ankara was named the capital of the newly formed Republic of Turkey.

In 2010, Istanbul was named the European Capital of Culture. By 2023, it had become the world's most visited city, attracting over 20 million international tourists, surpassing London and Dubai. Istanbul's historic center is a UNESCO World Heritage Site, and the

city remains a major economic hub, hosting the headquarters of numerous Turkish companies and contributing over 30% to the national economy.

Turkey's hospitality scene is as rich and varied as its culture. This chapter will guide you through the best places to stay in Turkey, helping you choose accommodations that align perfectly with your travel plans and style.

Best Areas to Stay in Istanbul

Istanbul, Turkey's largest city, offers an extraordinary blend of history, culture, and modernity. With its iconic landmarks, vibrant neighborhoods, and bustling bazaars, Istanbul is a city that never fails to captivate visitors. Each area caters to different traveler preferences, from history buffs to nightlife lovers.

➢ Sultanahmet

Sultanahmet is Istanbul's historical core, brimming with iconic landmarks like the Hagia Sophia, Blue Mosque, and Tokai Palace. It offers a deep dive into the city's Ottoman and Byzantine heritage. Accommodations here range from boutique hotels nestled in traditional Ottoman-style buildings to luxurious options with stunning views of the Bosphorus. The cobblestone streets, charming cafes, and proximity to historical sites make it an excellent choice for first-time visitors and history enthusiasts.

➢ Takis and Beyoğlu

Takis Square and Beyoğlu are the pulse of Istanbul's modern life, known for their bustling streets, vibrant nightlife, and cultural attractions. Itkila Avenue is a pedestrian paradise filled with shops, restaurants, and street performers, creating an electric atmosphere. Travelers staying here enjoy easy access to public transportation and a wide range of accommodation options, from budget hotels to upscale chains. The area also offers a mix of modern and historic attractions, including theaters, art galleries, and historical passages.

➢ Kaiky

Situated on Istanbul's Asian side, Kaiky provides a laid-back, authentic local experience. Known for its bustling markets, trendy cafes, and vibrant street art, it's a favorite for budget-conscious travelers seeking a bohemian vibe. The area is also famous for its food scene, offering everything from street food to gourmet restaurants. Staying in Kaiky provides a unique opportunity to enjoy ferry rides across the Bosphorus, offering stunning views of the city's skyline.

➢ Beşiktaş

Beşiktaş is a dynamic neighborhood that seamlessly blends culture, history, and modernity. It's home to the opulent Dominance Palace, high-end hotels, and trendy restaurants with scenic views of the Bosphorus. The lively fish market and waterfront promenade add to its charm, making it ideal for those seeking luxury and vibrant city life. Beşiktaş also offers excellent connectivity to other parts of Istanbul, making it a convenient base for exploration.

➢ Orakei

Orakei is a picturesque neighborhood famous for its waterfront setting, charming cafes, and the iconic Orakei Mosque, which sits majestically by the Bosphorus. It's a romantic area ideal for couples or travelers looking for a peaceful retreat. The area's boutique hotels offer spectacular views of the Bosphorus Bridge, especially at night when it's illuminated. Weekend markets and street food vendors selling bumper (stuffed baked potatoes) add to its unique charm.

➢ Galata

Galata, dominated by the historic Galata Tower, is a cultural hub filled with artistic energy. Its cobblestone streets are lined with boutique hotels, artisan shops, and trendy cafes. The area is perfect for travelers who appreciate history and culture, with easy access to the vibrant Karaoke district and the historic tram connecting it to Takis. Galata's panoramic views from the tower and its bohemian vibe make it a favorite for photographers and creatives.

➢ Sili

Sili is a modern district known for its skyscrapers, shopping malls, and business centers, catering primarily to business travelers and those seeking contemporary accommodations. It's a quieter alternative to Istanbul's bustling tourist hubs, offering a relaxed yet urban environment. With attractions like Cevahir Mall and several upscale hotels, Sili is also well-connected via public transport, making it an ideal choice for travelers who value convenience and modern amenities.

Best Hotels to Stay in Istanbul

Istanbul, a city that straddles two continents, is known for its stunning skyline, rich history, and vibrant culture. Whether you're visiting for leisure or business, Istanbul offers a range of accommodations that cater to every traveler's preference. From opulent palace hotels to chic boutique stays, here are some of the best hotels in Istanbul to consider for an unforgettable visit:

➤ Four Seasons Hotel Istanbul at the Bosphorus (Beşiktaş, European Side)

Set on the scenic banks of the Bosphorus, this luxurious hotel combines historical charm with modern elegance. Guests can enjoy spacious rooms adorned with Ottoman-inspired décor, an outdoor pool with waterfront views, and exceptional dining options. The hotel's tranquil spa and garden terrace make it a haven of relaxation in the bustling city.

➤ Caraan Palace Kempinski Istanbul (Orakei, European Side)

Housed in a 19th-century Ottoman palace, this iconic hotel epitomizes luxury. Its opulent rooms and suites, many of which overlook the Bosphorus, provide a royal experience. Guests can unwind in the infinity pool that appears to merge with the strait or indulge in fine dining at its renowned restaurants. The hotel's rich history and stunning architecture make it a standout choice.

➤ Raffles Istanbul (Zorlu Center, Beşiktaş)

Located within the prestigious Zorlu Center, Raffles Istanbul is a beacon of contemporary luxury. The hotel features spacious, stylish rooms with private terraces, an exquisite rooftop infinity pool, and a renowned spa offering signature treatments. Its proximity to upscale shopping and entertainment makes it perfect for modern travelers.

➤ The House Hotel Galata (Galata, Beyoğlu)

This boutique gem, situated near the historic Galata Tower, combines vintage charm with contemporary design. Its well-appointed rooms feature unique art and architecture inspired by Istanbul's history. The rooftop terrace offers stunning city views, while the hotel's central location provides easy access to local attractions and cultural landmarks.

➤ Pera Palace Hotel (Beyoğlu, European Side)

Steeped in history, Pera Palace is a legendary hotel that has hosted figures like Agatha Christie and Ernest Hemingway. Its lavish rooms reflect the grandeur of its past while offering modern comforts. Guests can enjoy the iconic tea lounge, elegant dining options, and a glimpse into Istanbul's literary and cultural heritage.

➤ The Bank Hotel Istanbul (Karaoke, European Side)

Located in the trendy Karaoke district, this hotel occupies a beautifully restored 19th-century bank building. Its chic, modern rooms feature sleek design elements, while the rooftop terrace provides panoramic views of the city and Bosphorus. The on-site restaurant offers a creative menu inspired by Mediterranean flavors.

➤ InterContinental Istanbul (Takis, European Side)

Set in the vibrant Takis district, this upscale hotel is ideal for both business and leisure travelers. The elegant rooms offer stunning views of the Bosphorus or city skyline. Guests can savor gourmet

Turkish cuisine, relax in the spa, or enjoy cocktails at the rooftop bar. Its central location makes exploring Istanbul effortless.

➤ Hilton Istanbul Bosphorus (Herbie, Sili)

This landmark hotel is nestled within lush gardens, providing a serene escape in the heart of the city. The Hilton features a variety of room options, many with private balconies and Bosphorus views. Guests can enjoy multiple dining venues, a luxurious spa, and indoor and outdoor pools.

➤ Swissotel The Bosphorus Istanbul (Beşiktaş, European Side)

A luxurious urban resort, Swissotel offers unparalleled views of the Bosphorus Strait and city skyline. Its modern rooms are complemented by an award-winning spa, an outdoor infinity pool, and gourmet restaurants serving global and Turkish cuisine. The hotel's central location provides easy access to major landmarks.

➤ The St. Regis Istanbul (Nantais, European Side)

Located in Istanbul's high-end shopping district, this sophisticated hotel combines timeless elegance with contemporary luxury. Guests can enjoy personalized butler service, opulent rooms, and a Michelin-starred rooftop restaurant and bar. Its location in Nishanta's makes it an excellent choice for fashion and art lovers.

Whether you prefer historic charm or modern sophistication, these hotels offer unparalleled service, amenities, and locations that enhance any visit to Istanbul. From iconic landmarks to vibrant neighborhoods, your stay will be as memorable as the city itself.

Best Places to Visit in Istanbul

➤ Hagia Sophia

A masterpiece of Byzantine architecture, the Hagia Sophia stands as a symbol of Istanbul's layered history. Built in 537 ADS, its massive dome and intricate mosaics reflect the grandeur of the Byzantine Empire. Once a church, then a mosque, and now a museum, it showcases a blend of Christian and Islamic art and architecture. Visitors can marvel at the massive central nave, climb to the upper galleries for a closer view of ancient mosaics, and imagine the echoes of centuries-old prayers in this awe-inspiring monument.

➤ Blue Mosque

Known officially as the Sultan Ahmed Mosque, the Blue Mosque is an architectural jewel of the Ottoman era. Completed in 1616, it is named after the over 20,000 hand-painted blue Biznik tiles that adorn its interior walls. Its six minarets, spacious courtyard, and cascading domes make it one of the most iconic landmarks in Istanbul. Visitors can explore its serene interiors during non-prayer hours and admire the intricate floral and geometric designs that reflect the zenith of Ottoman artistry.

➤ Tokai Palace

As the residence of Ottoman sultans for nearly 400 years, Tokai Palace is a treasure trove of history and opulence. Spanning over 700,000 square meters, the complex includes courtyards, lush gardens, and ornate pavilions. Inside, visitors can view the Imperial Treasury's priceless jewels, the Prophet Muhammad's sacred relics in the Chamber of Holy Relics, and the luxurious Harem quarters, where the sultan's family lived. Each corner of the palace tells tales of intrigue, grandeur, and empire.

➤ Grand Bazaar (Kapali Caris)

One of the oldest and largest covered markets in the world, the Grand Bazaar is a vibrant labyrinth of over 4,000 shops. Established in the 15th century, it is a hub for trading Turkish carpets, gold jewelry, leather goods, spices, and souvenirs. Its colorful atmosphere, bustling energy, and historic charm make it an unforgettable shopping experience. Visitors can wander through its vaulted passages, bargain for unique items, and soak in the rich cultural tapestry of Istanbul's market life.

➢ Basilica Cistern

Built in the 6th century during Emperor Justinian's reign, the Basilica Cistern is an underground marvel. This massive cistern, capable of holding 80,000 cubic meters of water, features 336 marble columns arranged in a grid pattern. Its dimly lit interior, the sound of dripping water, and the mysterious Medusa head carvings create an otherworldly ambiance. Visitors often describe walking through this ancient water reservoir as a step back in time to Byzantium's engineering brilliance.

➢ Galata Tower

A defining feature of Istanbul's skyline, the Galata Tower offers unparalleled views of the city. Originally built in 1348 as part of the Genoese fortifications, this cylindrical stone tower has served various purposes over the centuries, from a watchtower to a fire observatory. Today, visitors can ascend to its observation deck for breathtaking panoramas of the Golden Horn, Bosphorus, and historic districts. It's also a great spot to watch the sunset over Istanbul.

➢ Bosphorus Strait

This iconic waterway separates the European and Asian sides of Istanbul, making it one of the city's most scenic and significant landmarks. A boat cruise along the Bosphorus offers stunning views of waterfront mansions, historic fortresses like Rumelia

Hisar, and Ottoman palaces such as Dominance and Beylerbey. Sunset cruises are particularly popular, as the water reflects the golden hues of the setting sun, creating a magical atmosphere.

➤ Dominance Palace

A symbol of Ottoman modernization, Dominance Palace was constructed in the mid-19th century. Its blend of European architectural styles, such as Baroque, Rococo, and Neoclassical, showcases the empire's efforts to align with Western trends. Visitors can admire the opulent interiors, including the Grand Ceremonial Hall with its 4.5-ton chandelier, and explore the vast gardens overlooking the Bosphorus.

➤ Chora Church (Kariya Museum)

This lesser-known gem is a haven for art and history lovers. Famous for its well-preserved Byzantine mosaics and frescoes, the Chora Church narrates biblical stories in exquisite detail. Tucked away in the Edirne Kapi district, its serene ambiance and artistic beauty provide a stark contrast to Istanbul's bustling streets, making it a must-visit site.

➤ Spice Bazaar (Miser Carissa)

Bursting with colors and aromas, the Spice Bazaar in Eminent has been a center of trade since the 17th century. It offers an array of spices, dried fruits, nuts, Turkish delights, and teas, alongside souvenirs like ceramics and textiles. The bazaar is a sensory delight and an ideal place for foodies to explore Istanbul's culinary heritage.

➢ Hippodrome of Constantinople

Once the social and sporting hub of Byzantine Constantinople, the Hippodrome hosted chariot races and grand celebrations. Today, it's a public square (Sultanahmet Meydan) adorned with historical monuments like the Obelisk of Theodosius, the Serpent Column, and the German Fountain. Walking through the Hippodrome offers a glimpse into the grandeur of Byzantium.

➢ Sulaymaniyah Mosque

Commissioned by Sultan Suleiman the Magnificent and designed by the renowned architect Sinan, the Sulaymaniyah Mosque is a masterpiece of Ottoman architecture. Perched on a hill, it offers stunning views of the Golden Horn. Its serene interior, intricate tilework, and beautifully landscaped courtyard make it a peaceful retreat from the city's hustle.

➢ Rumelia Fortress (Rumelia Hisar)

Strategically located on the European side of the Bosphorus, Rumelia Fortress was built in just four months in 1452 to aid the Ottoman conquest of Constantinople. Its imposing towers and walls are well-preserved, and the fortress now serves as a museum and venue for summer concerts. The site offers stunning views of the Bosphorus and insight into military history.

➢ Pierre Loti Hill

Named after the French writer who frequented this spot, Pierre Loti Hill offers tranquil surroundings and breathtaking views of the

Golden Horn. Visitors can enjoy a traditional Turkish tea or coffee at the hilltop café while soaking in the panoramic vistas. A cable car ride adds a fun and scenic way to access the hill.

➢ Itkila Avenue (Itkila Caddes)

Stretching from Takis Square to Galata Tower, Itkila Avenue is Istanbul's most famous pedestrian street. It's a vibrant hub of activity, lined with shops, cafes, art galleries, and historical landmarks. The nostalgic tram that runs along the avenue adds to its charm, making it a must-visit for shopping and cultural exploration.

Best Restaurants in Istanbul

Istanbul's culinary scene is a fusion of flavors influenced by its rich history, diverse cultures, and vibrant local ingredients. From traditional Turkish eateries to world-class fine dining, the city offers a range of dining experiences that cater to all tastes. Here are some of the best restaurants you should try when in Istanbul:

➢ Nusra-Et Steakhouse (Eiler, Beşiktaş)

Nusra-Et Steakhouse, located in Eiler, Beşiktaş, has gained worldwide fame for its high-quality cuts of meat and the signature "Salt Bae" experience. This trendy and upscale eatery is a favorite for meat lovers who want to indulge in perfectly cooked steaks, burgers, and decadent sides. With multiple locations worldwide, this is one spot in Istanbul that meat enthusiasts cannot miss.

➤ Mikla (Pera, Beyoğlu)

Perched atop The Marmara Pera hotel in Beyoğlu, Mikla combines modern Turkish cuisine with Scandinavian influences. This Michelin-recognized restaurant offers innovative dishes with seasonal ingredients while providing panoramic views of Istanbul's skyline, especially at sunset. A perfect mix of elegance, creativity, and great food makes Mikla a must-visit for gastronomes.

➤ Çiya Sonrais (Kaiky)

Located in Kaiky on the Asian side of Istanbul, Çiya Sonrais is a legendary restaurant that showcases the diverse and rich flavors of Anatolian cuisine. Known for its wide selection of dishes from various Turkish regions, it offers everything from savory stews to unique mezes, all crafted with traditional techniques and fresh ingredients. It's a beloved spot among locals and travelers for an authentic taste of Turkish heritage.

➢ Neolocal (Karaoke)

Neolocal, located in the heart of Karaoke, is a Michelin-starred restaurant that takes traditional Turkish recipes and gives them a modern and innovative twist. Led by chef Makrut Askar, it focuses on sustainability and using locally sourced ingredients. With an ever-evolving menu and a strong emphasis on creativity, Neolocal is a perfect choice for those seeking a contemporary approach to Turkish cuisine.

➢ Karaoke Locants (Karaoke)

Karaoke locants, situated in the vibrant karaoke district, is known for its chic décor and its delicious mezze offerings. The restaurant blends modern design with traditional flavors, serving a variety of dishes from both Turkish and Mediterranean cuisines. The ambiance, paired with flavorful dishes and top-notch service, makes it a popular spot for both locals and tourists.

➢ Tarini Sultanahmet Kutaisi (Sultanahmet)

Located near the iconic Blue Mosque, Tarini Sultanahmet Kutaisi has been serving its signature Turkish meatballs (kofta) for decades. It's a simple yet beloved institution, offering kofta served with Turkish-style rice, picas (bean salad), and fresh bread. A must-try for anyone looking to enjoy a quintessentially Turkish meal in the heart of Istanbul's historic district.

➢ Ulus 29 (Ulus, Beşiktaş)

Nestled in the upscale district of Ulus, Ulus 29 is an elegant restaurant offering a blend of Turkish and international cuisine with an emphasis on fresh, seasonal ingredients. The sophisticated setting includes breathtaking views of the Bosphorus, creating a luxurious dining experience. Whether you're looking for a romantic dinner or a refined night out, Ulus 29 promises both delicious food and stunning vistas.

➢ Samali Cavit (Beyoğlu)

Amali Cavit, located in the lively Amali Mesquit Street in Beyoğlu, is a traditional methane (Turkish tavern) that serves a variety of homemade mezes and fresh fish. With a rustic charm and a warm, welcoming atmosphere, this restaurant is a favorite for those looking to experience authentic Turkish meze dining. Pair your meal with a glass of raki, the national drink, for the full experience.

➢ 360 Istanbul (Beyoğlu)

360 Istanbul, perched on the rooftop of a historic building in Beyoğlu, offers not just a meal, but an experience. Known for its international cuisine with a Turkish twist, the restaurant serves a selection of creative cocktails and modern dishes with a stunning 360-degree view of Istanbul. It's perfect for enjoying a meal while taking in a breathtaking view of the city at night.

➢ Meze by Lemon Tree (Beyoğlu)

Located in the trendy district of Beyoğlu, Meze by Lemon Tree is a modern restaurant that reinterprets traditional Turkish mezes with an elegant, contemporary flair. The restaurant offers a chic atmosphere, exquisite flavors, and an exceptional wine list, making it a popular choice for those looking for a refined yet relaxed dining experience.

Istanbul's diverse dining scene is a reflection of its rich history, offering a variety of options that appeal to all tastes. Whether you're craving traditional Turkish dishes or a more modern culinary adventure, Istanbul's best restaurants promise to deliver unforgettable dining experiences.

Best Shopping Centers in Istanbul

Istanbul is a shopper's paradise, blending the charm of ancient markets with the allure of modern malls. From historic bazaars to luxurious shopping complexes, the city offers something for every kind of shopper. Here's a detailed look at some of the best shopping destinations in Istanbul:

➢ Grand Bazaar (Kapali Caris, Beast)

Located in the heart of the Old City in Beast, the Grand Bazaar is one of the oldest and largest covered markets in the world, with over 4,000 shops. A labyrinth of stalls offers everything from handmade carpets and gold jewelry to ceramics and antiques. The bazaar is not just a shopping destination but an iconic cultural experience steeped in history and tradition.

➢ Sistine Park (Seroyer, European Side)

Situated in the upscale Seroyer district, Sistine Park is a luxurious shopping mall boasting a mix of high-end international brands such as Louis Vuitton and Gucci alongside Turkish designers. The mall features an open-air shopping area, a gourmet food market, and an IMAX theater. It's a must-visit for fashionistas and families looking for a stylish shopping experience.

➢ Zorlu Center (Beşiktaş, European Side)

Zorlu Center in Beşiktaş combines luxury and entertainment with designer stores like Dior, Valentino, and Burberry, alongside fine dining options and a state-of-the-art performing arts theater. This modern mall is also home to one of Istanbul's most Instagram-worthy Apple Stores and hosts cultural events, making it more than just a shopping destination.

➤ Emaar Square Mall (Sukumar, Asian Side)

Located in Sukumar on the Asian side, Emaar Square Mall is a blend of international and Turkish brands. In addition to retail therapy, visitors can explore an aquarium, an observation deck with panoramic city views, and a variety of dining options. This family-friendly mall also has a kid's entertainment area, making it perfect for a day out.

➤ Cevahir Mall (Sili, European Side)

Known as one of the largest malls in Europe, Cevahir Mall in Sili offers a wide array of retail stores, from global brands like Zara and Mango to Turkish retailers. It also features a large food court, a cinema complex, and even amusement park rides, ensuring entertainment for all ages. Its central location and extensive offerings make it a popular choice for visitors.

➤ Kanyon Mall (Levent, European Side)

Famous for its unique open-air architectural design, Kanyon Mall in Levent provides a modern shopping experience. It offers a curated selection of retail stores, upscale restaurants, and cafes, making it a hub for trendsetters. The mall's vibrant ambiance and stylish atmosphere attract both locals and tourists looking for something chic and contemporary.

➤ Spice Bazaar (Miser Carissa, Eminent)

Nestled near the New Mosque in Eminent, the Spice Bazaar is a feast for the senses. It's the perfect spot for purchasing aromatic spices, dried fruits, nuts, and traditional Turkish delights. The bazaar has been a bustling marketplace since the 17th century, and its lively atmosphere makes it a must-see for visitors.

➤ Akasya Mall (Academe, Asian Side)

Located in Academe on the Asian side, Akasya Mall is known for its spacious layout and variety of stores, including premium brands like Apple, Victoria's Secret, and Hugo Boss. It also has a gourmet dining area, a large entertainment zone for kids, and a luxurious cinema experience. It's an excellent destination for family outings or high-end shopping.

➤ Forum Istanbul (Bayram Pasa, European Side)

Forum Istanbul in Bayram Pasa is one of the largest malls in the city, featuring a vast range of retail stores, IKEA, and unique attractions like Sea Life Aquarium. It's a family-friendly venue offering activities for all ages, including a bowling alley and a cinema. Its convenient location near public transport makes it easy to visit.

➤ City's Nishanta's (Nishanta's, Sili)

Situated in the trendy Nishanta's district, City's Mall is an upscale shopping center offering boutique stores, luxury brands, and a stylish food court. Known for its elegant atmosphere, the mall caters to a fashionable crowd and is surrounded by charming streets filled with cafes and local designer shops.

Istanbul's shopping scene seamlessly blends the old and the new, offering a unique experience that caters to both bargain hunters and luxury seekers. Whether you're looking for local handicrafts or high-end fashion, these shopping centers and markets are sure to leave you with cherished memories and plenty of souvenirs.

Nightlife in Istanbul

Istanbul's vibrant nightlife reflects the city's unique blend of cultures, offering an array of options ranging from high-energy nightclubs to cozy bars and cultural music venues. Whether you prefer panoramic rooftop views or dancing the night away by the Bosphorus, Istanbul's nightlife has something for everyone. Here's a look at the city's top nightlife spots:

➢ Sortie (Orakei, European Side)

Set along the Bosphorus in Orakei, Sortie is a glamorous nightclub and restaurant complex known for its breathtaking waterfront views, exceptional cocktails, and lively DJ performances. The venue offers multiple dining options and transforms into a pulsating dance floor after dark, making it a favorite among locals and visitors seeking an upscale party experience.

➢ 360 Istanbul (Itkila Street, Beyoğlu)

Perched atop a historic building on Itkila Street, 360 Istanbul is a chic rooftop bar and restaurant offering panoramic views of Istanbul's skyline. Known for its eclectic menu and creative cocktails, the venue hosts a variety of events, including live music and DJ sets, making it a versatile spot for dinner, drinks, and late-night revelry.

➤ **Babylon (Belontiid, Sili)**

Located in the hip cultural hub of Belontiid, Babylon is a renowned live music venue featuring performances by jazz, indie, and world music artists. With its intimate atmosphere and diverse lineup, it's a favorite among music enthusiasts and offers an alternative to the typical nightclub experience.

➤ **Ruby (Orakei, European Side)**

Nestled along the Bosphorus in Orakei, Ruby is a hotspot for upscale nightlife. With its stunning waterside location, trendy décor, and energetic atmosphere, Ruby is the perfect destination for high-energy parties. It boasts a chic crowd, top-notch drinks, and international DJs that keep the party going all night.

➤ Arcada (Kaiky, Asian Side)

Hidden in the artsy Kaiky district, Arcada offers a relaxed vibe with an indie twist. Known for its alternative music scene and diverse events, including experimental DJ sets and live performances, this cozy venue is a haven for those seeking a more laid-back and creative nightlife experience.

➤ Riti (Takis, Beyoğlu)

Riti is a lively spot located in the heart of Takis, famous for its Turkish music nights. The venue combines traditional and modern beats, making it a great place to experience Istanbul's local music culture while enjoying drinks and mingling with a spirited crowd.

➤ Ulus 29 Club (Ulus, Beşiktaş)

Known for its fine dining and lively club atmosphere, Ulus 29 offers an elegant nightlife experience. Set atop a hill in Ulus, the venue provides stunning views of the Bosphorus. After dinner, it transitions into a chic club with great music, attracting an upscale and fashionable crowd.

➤ Klein (Herbie, Sili)

Klein is a trendy nightclub located in Herbie, Sili, known for its underground electronic music scene and artistic ambiance. The venue features cutting-edge lighting and sound systems, drawing a young and creative crowd. It's a go-to spot for fans of techno and house music.

➤ Nardis Jazz Club (Galata, Beyoğlu)

Tucked away near the iconic Galata Tower, Nardis Jazz Club is an intimate venue showcasing top-notch live jazz performances. Ideal for a relaxed evening, the club attracts both locals and tourists with its world-class musicians and cozy atmosphere, offering a quieter alternative to the city's high-energy nightlife.

➤ Supperclub Istanbul (Levent, European Side)

Located in Levent, Supperclub Istanbul combines fine dining with high-energy entertainment. Known for its immersive performances, extravagant shows, and stylish décor, it provides a unique nightlife experience. As the evening progresses, the venue transforms into a vibrant nightclub with DJs spinning diverse genres.

Istanbul's nightlife offers a mix of tradition and modernity, catering to all preferences. Whether you're looking for a lavish party by the Bosphorus or a cozy music venue in a bohemian neighborhood, Istanbul promises unforgettable evenings.

Exploring Istanbul in 7 Days

Istanbul is a city where history, culture, and modernity blend seamlessly. A seven-day itinerary lets you dive deep into its treasures, from ancient landmarks to vibrant neighborhoods, without feeling rushed. Here's a detailed plan for your week in this enchanting city:

Day 1: Arrival and Initial Exploration in Istanbul

- **Morning**

Upon arrival in Istanbul, settle into your hotel and start your journey with a traditional Turkish breakfast at a local café. Treat yourself to a variety of delicacies, including simit (sesame-covered bread), mermen (Turkish-style scrambled eggs), fresh cheeses, olives, and sweet honey. This meal will energize you for your first day of exploration in this vibrant city.

- **Afternoon**

Take a leisurely stroll through Sultanahmet Square, the heart of Istanbul's historic district. Explore the Hippodrome, once a grand arena for chariot races, and marvel at its ancient monuments, including the Obelisk of Theodosius and the Serpent Column.

- **Evening**

Dine at a cozy restaurant near the Blue Mosque and savor Turkish kebabs, mezes, or pied (Turkish pizza). After dinner, enjoy a serene walk around Sultanahmet Square, where the illuminated domes and minarets of Hagia Sophia and the Blue Mosque create a magical atmosphere.

Day 2: Sultanahmet – The Historic Core

- **Morning**

Begin your day at Hagia Sophia, one of the world's most iconic architectural masterpieces. Marvel at its vast dome, intricate mosaics, and centuries of history as both a church and a mosque. Next, step into the serene Blue Mosque, famous for its six minarets and breathtaking Biznik tiles that decorate the interior.

- **Afternoon**

Visit Tokai Palace, once the opulent residence of Ottoman Sultans. Wander through its sprawling courtyards, explore the Harem for a glimpse into royal life, and admire its vast collection of treasures, including the dazzling Tokai Dagger and the Spoon maker's Diamond.

- **Evening**

Treat yourself to dinner at a traditional Ottoman-style restaurant nearby. Afterward, take a quiet stroll through the streets around the Basilica Cistern, soaking in the peaceful nighttime ambiance.

Day 3: Shopping and Local Experiences

- **Morning**

Dive into the bustling energy of the Grand Bazaar, one of the world's oldest and largest covered markets. Explore its labyrinthine alleys filled with shops offering Turkish carpets, hand-painted ceramics, exquisite jewelry, and artisanal goods. Bargaining is part of the experience, so don't hesitate to negotiate!

- **Afternoon**

Head to the Spice Bazaar in Eminent, a sensory delight with its vibrant displays of spices, dried fruits, teas, and Turkish delights. From here, take a ferry to the Asian side of Istanbul and wander through the lively Kaiky Market, where you'll find fresh produce, street food, and unique local products.

- **Evening**

Return to the European side for dinner at a seafood restaurant along the Galata Bridge. Savor fresh fish or mezes while enjoying views of the shimmering Bosphorus.

Day 4: Bosphorus Cruise and Palaces

- **Morning**

Begin your day with a tour of Dominance Palace, a magnificent 19th-century palace that served as the Ottoman Empire's administrative center. Marvel at its opulent interiors, including the grand staircase, massive crystal chandeliers, and intricately decorated halls.

- **Afternoon**

Embark on a scenic Bosphorus cruise, where you can admire the city's stunning skyline, waterfront mansions, and iconic landmarks like the Bosphorus Bridge. Learn about the history of the strait that separates Europe and Asia while soaking in the breathtaking views.

- **Evening**

Disembark at Orakei, a charming neighborhood along the Bosphorus. Try a plate of **bumper** (stuffed baked potato with various toppings) and stroll through its lively streets filled with shops and cafes. End your day with a tea or coffee by the water.

Day 5: Beyoğlu and Galata

- **Morning**

Start your day with a visit to Galata Tower, a medieval stone tower that offers panoramic views of Istanbul. From here, wander through the historic streets of Galata, home to charming boutiques, art galleries, and trendy cafes.

- **Afternoon**

Explore Itkila Avenue, a bustling pedestrian street lined with shops, restaurants, and historic buildings. Don't miss the chance to ride the historic red tram or stop by the Pera Museum to admire its art collection and cultural exhibitions.

- **Evening**

Enjoy dinner at a rooftop restaurant in Takis Square, where you can dine on Turkish and international cuisine while taking in views of the Bosphorus. If you're in the mood for nightlife, head to one of the area's chic bars or live music venues for a memorable evening.

Day 6: Off-the-Beaten-Path Adventures

- **Morning**

Visit Chora Church (Kariya Museum), a hidden gem renowned for its stunning Byzantine mosaics and frescoes that depict biblical scenes with intricate detail and vibrant colors.

- **Afternoon**

Explore the colorful neighborhoods of Balta and Fener, known for their narrow cobblestone streets, brightly painted houses, and unique cafes. Stop by the historic Greek Orthodox Patriarchate Church and browse through local antique shops and artisan stores.

- **Evening**

Take the cable car up to Pierre Loti Hill, a peaceful escape overlooking the Golden Horn. Relax with a cup of Turkish tea or coffee as you watch the sunset and take in the stunning views of Istanbul's skyline.

Day 7: Relaxation and Farewell

- **Morning**

Take a ferry to Bayada, the largest of the Princes' Islands, for a tranquil day away from the city's hustle and bustle. Rent a bike or walk through the island's peaceful streets, lined with charming wooden mansions and surrounded by lush greenery.

- **Afternoon**

Return to Istanbul and spend your final hours shopping for souvenirs at Sistine Park or exploring the upscale boutiques of Nishanta's.

- **Evening**

End your trip with a rejuvenating Turkish bath at a historic hammam, such as Catalogue Hammam or Sulaymaniyah Hammam. Enjoy the soothing experience before heading to the airport, leaving Istanbul refreshed and filled with unforgettable memories.

.... Enjoy Istanbul.....

CHAPTER 4

ANTALYA

Did you know Antalya is nicknamed the "Turkish Riviera" for its stunning Mediterranean coastline and luxury appeal?

This coastal gem blends ancient history, natural beauty, and modern charm, making it one of Turkey's most captivating destinations. From the cobblestone streets of Kalelike to the turquoise waters of Lara Beach, Antalya offers unforgettable experiences for every traveler.

Antalya, Turkey's fifth-largest city and the capital of Antalya Province, is a major hub for tourism and a key part of the Turkish Riviera. Nestled along the Mediterranean Sea on Anatolia's southwest coast and backed by the Taurus Mountains, Antalya is home to over 2.6 million residents, making it the largest city in Turkey's Mediterranean region. Often referred to as the "capital of tourism," Antalya boasts a unique blend of natural beauty, history, and modern appeal.

Originally known as Attalia, the city was founded around 200 BC by King Attalus II of Pergamon. It later came under Roman rule, during which it flourished, seeing the construction of landmarks like Hadrian's Gate and the prosperity of nearby ancient cities such as Patara, Xanthos, and Myra in Lycia, as well as Perga, Aspen Dos, and Side in Pamphylia. Over the centuries, Antalya changed hands multiple times, becoming part of the Seljuk Empire in 1207 and the Ottoman Empire in 1391. Ottoman rule ushered in a period of stability that lasted for 500 years. After briefly falling under Italian occupation following World War I, the city was reclaimed during the Turkish War of Independence.

Geographically, while Antalya itself experiences mild elevation changes, it is surrounded by high mountains. This unique setting traps moisture, resulting in significant winter rainfall, while the bay's location contributes to its scorching summer temperatures.

Today, Antalya stands as Turkey's largest international sea resort and a centerpiece of the Turkish Riviera. Government investment and extensive development have solidified its status as a top global destination. In 2023, Antalya ranked as the world's fourth-most visited city, attracting over 16.5 million international tourists, surpassed only by Istanbul, London, and Dubai.

Best Areas to Stay in Antalya

Antalya, the crown jewel of Turkey's Mediterranean coast, offers a diverse range of accommodations, from historic old-town stays to luxurious beachfront resorts. Its stunning beaches, ancient ruins, vibrant nightlife, and natural beauty make it a destination that caters to all types of travelers. Here's a detailed look at the best areas to stay in Antalya, ensuring your visit is perfectly tailored to your preferences.

> ### Kalelike (Old Town)

Kalelike, Antalya's historic heart, is a must-visit for travelers who love history and charm. This area is a maze of cobblestone streets, Ottoman-era mansions, and picturesque courtyards. The historic harbor, once a hub for traders and merchants, is now lined with cafes and restaurants offering stunning views of the Mediterranean.

➤ Lara Beach

Lara Beach is famous for its long stretches of golden sand and a collection of high-end, all-inclusive resorts. The area caters to families and beach lovers, offering a mix of water sports, entertainment, and relaxation. Its proximity to Antalya Airport makes it a convenient choice for travelers looking to maximize their beach time.

➤ Konya alti

Konya alti is perfect for travelers looking for a blend of natural beauty and modern amenities. Its expansive pebble beach stretches for kilometers, backed by the striking Taurus Mountains. This area offers a more relaxed vibe compared to Lara Beach and has plenty of attractions nearby.

➢ Belek

Belek is synonymous with luxury and leisure, boasting world-class golf courses, high-end resorts, and wellness facilities. The area is a haven for golfers, offering pristine courses designed by renowned architects. Beyond golf, Belek's resorts focus on tranquility, with spa treatments, fine dining, and private beaches.

➢ Side

Side seamlessly combines ancient history with modern beach life. The town is home to remarkable Greco-Roman ruins, including the Temple of Apollo, which overlooks the sea. Side's vibrant promenade is lined with restaurants and cafes, offering stunning views of the coastline.

➢ Kemer

Kemer is a coastal paradise nestled between the Taurus Mountains and the sparkling Mediterranean. Known for its stunning natural beauty, Kemer offers a blend of adventure, luxury, and vibrant nightlife. Its turquoise waters and pine-clad hills create a picture-perfect setting.

➢ Alanya

Located further east of Antalya, Alanya is a lively destination with something for everyone. Its sandy beaches, historic landmarks, and vibrant nightlife make it a popular choice for families and young travelers alike. The town's iconic Alanya Castle offers breathtaking views of the coast.

Antalya's diverse regions ensure that every traveler, whether seeking history, luxury, adventure, or relaxation, will find their perfect stay. With its breathtaking landscapes, rich cultural heritage, and exceptional hospitality, Antalya is a destination that leaves a lasting impression.

Best Hotels to Stay in Antalya

Antalya, a premier destination on Turkey's Mediterranean coast, offers a diverse array of accommodations to suit various preferences and budgets. Here's an overview of some notable hotels in the region:

➢ Akra Antalya

Situated along the Mediterranean coastline, Akra Antalya is a luxurious hotel renowned for its stunning sea views and exceptional amenities. Guests can indulge in a world-class spa, multiple gourmet restaurants, and enjoy direct access to a private beach. The hotel also features indoor and outdoor pools, a rooftop terrace, and a fitness center, catering to both relaxation and active pursuits.

➢ Rios Downtown Antalya

Located in the heart of Antalya, Ricos Downtown Antalya combines modern design with comfort. The hotel boasts a rooftop pool offering panoramic views, a full-service spa, and several fine dining options. Its central location provides easy access to the city's attractions, making it an ideal choice for travelers seeking both luxury and convenience.

> ## Crowne Plaza Antalya

This contemporary hotel offers comfortable rooms equipped with modern amenities. Guests can choose from a variety of dining options and utilize the on-site fitness center. The hotel's proximity to the beach and city center makes it a convenient base for exploring Antalya.

> ## Alp Paca Hotel

Nestled in the historic Kaliese district, Alp Paca Hotel is a boutique establishment characterized by its elegant rooms and authentic Ottoman architecture. Guests can enjoy the rooftop terrace, which provides views of the old town, and dine in the hotel's restaurant that offers traditional Turkish cuisine.

➢ Sherwood Exclusive Lara

An all-inclusive resort, Sherwood Exclusive Lara features multiple pools, a private beach, and a wide range of activities suitable for all ages. The resort offers various dining venues, entertainment options, and recreational facilities, ensuring a comprehensive vacation experience.

➢ Lara Barut Collection

This upscale all-inclusive resort boasts a spa, water park, and numerous dining options. Guests can enjoy spacious rooms, extensive leisure facilities, and personalized services, making it a popular choice for families and couples alike.

➢ IC Hotels Airport

Conveniently located near Antalya Airport, IC Hotels Airport offers modern rooms, a spa, and a rooftop bar. It's an ideal option for travelers seeking accommodation close to the airport without compromising on comfort and amenities.

➢ Hotel SU & Aqualand

A family-friendly resort, Hotel SU & Aqualand features a water park, spa, and multiple dining options. Its minimalist design and extensive facilities cater to both relaxation and entertainment, appealing to guests of all ages.

➤ Mega Saray West beach Antalya

This luxurious resort offers a private beach, spa, and a wide range of activities. Guests can enjoy elegantly designed rooms, diverse dining options, and recreational facilities that cater to both adults and children.

➤ Sealife Family Resort Hotel

Designed with families in mind, Sealife Family Resort Hotel includes a water park, spa, and various dining venues. Its family-friendly amenities and proximity to the beach make it a favored choice for those traveling with children.

➤ Titanic Deluxe Lara

An all-inclusive resort, Titanic Deluxe Lara features a private beach, spa, and a multitude of activities. Its unique design, inspired by the Titanic ship, along with its extensive facilities, provides a memorable vacation experience.

When selecting accommodation in Antalya, consider factors such as location, amenities, and the type of experience you desire to ensure a satisfying stay.

Best Places to Visit in Antalya

➤ Antalya Old Town (Kaliese)

Kaliese, the heart of Antalya's history, charms visitors with its labyrinth of cobblestone streets and Ottoman-era architecture. Lined with quaint shops, boutique hotels, and cozy cafes, the district offers a picturesque blend of culture and comfort. The historic harbor, a bustling focal point, is perfect for leisurely walks or scenic boat tours. Kaliese seamlessly merges Antalya's ancient past with vibrant modern life, making it an unforgettable destination.

➢ Hadrian's Gate

Hadrian's Gate, a masterpiece of Roman architecture built in 130 CE, stands as a grand entrance to Kaliese. Adorned with ornate carvings and marble columns, this triumphal arch was constructed to honor Emperor Hadrian's visit. Walking beneath its ancient arches feels like stepping back in time. Surrounded by modern

Antalya, it's a poignant reminder of the city's layered history and cultural significance.

➤ Deden Waterfalls

The Deden Waterfalls are Antalya's natural wonders, offering serene beauty and dramatic landscapes. The Upper Deden, set amidst lush greenery, is a tranquil retreat with picnic areas and caves to explore. The Lower Deden captivates with its powerful cascade plunging into the Mediterranean, creating a striking coastal spectacle. Both sites provide breathtaking views and are perfect for nature lovers and photographers alike.

➤ Konya alti Beach

Konya alti Beach stretches along Antalya's turquoise coastline, inviting visitors to relax or engage in water sports. Surrounded by the majestic Taurus Mountains, the beach is complemented by nearby parks and cafes, offering something for everyone. Its clean, pebbled shoreline and calm waters make it ideal for families and adventure seekers. Konya alti's blend of natural beauty and recreational amenities ensures an unforgettable seaside experience.

➤ Perge Ancient City

Perge, an archaeological treasure, unveils the grandeur of ancient Roman and Greek civilizations. Visitors can wander through its remarkably preserved stadium, theater, and column-lined avenues. Once a vibrant trade hub, Perge reflects the artistic and architectural brilliance of its time. Located just outside Antalya, this historic site offers a captivating journey into the region's rich past, perfect for history buffs and cultural explorers.

➢ Aspen Dos Ancient Theater

The Aspen Dos Theater, a Roman engineering marvel, boasts a capacity of 15,000 and exceptional acoustics. Constructed in 155 CE, it remains one of the best-preserved theaters globally and still hosts cultural events. Surrounded by verdant hills, the site offers a glimpse into the grandeur of Roman entertainment. Whether exploring its detailed carvings or attending a live performance, Aspen Dos is a cultural highlight near Antalya.

➢ Side Ancient City

Side, a coastal gem, harmonizes historical ruins with Mediterranean charm. Visitors can explore landmarks such as the Temple of Apollo and a Roman theater, while enjoying stunning seaside views. The town's bustling promenade features shops, cafes, and markets that blend modernity with tradition. Whether savoring its ancient allure or vibrant atmosphere, Side offers a unique mix of history and relaxation.

➢ Köprülü Canyon National Park

Köprülü Canyon National Park enchants with its rugged cliffs, turquoise waters, and lush greenery. Adventure seekers can enjoy activities like rafting along the Kaprice River or hiking its scenic trails. The park also features ancient Roman bridges and diverse flora and fauna. Perfect for nature enthusiasts and thrill-seekers, this park is a breathtaking escape into Antalya's wild side, offering unforgettable outdoor experiences.

➢ **Kurkul Waterfalls**

Tucked within a tranquil forest, Kurkul Waterfalls cascade into emerald pools, creating a serene natural retreat. Accessible via scenic trails, the falls are surrounded by lush vegetation and vibrant wildlife. Visitors can enjoy picnicking, photography, or simply soaking in the peaceful ambiance. Kurkul's enchanting setting makes it a favorite for those seeking a quiet escape amid Antalya's natural beauty.

➢ **Antalya Aquarium**

Antalya Aquarium offers a mesmerizing journey through the underwater world, housing diverse marine species in creatively themed exhibits. Highlights include the world's longest tunnel aquarium and interactive experiences like feeding sessions. Perfect for families, it combines education and entertainment, providing an immersive marine adventure. Located near Konya alti Beach, it's an engaging destination for visitors of all ages.

➢ **Yilin Minaret Mosque**

The Yilin Minaret Mosque, built in the 13th century, is a stunning example of Seljuk architecture. Its iconic fluted minaret, visible from miles away, has become a symbol of Antalya. The mosque complex also includes historic structures like a medrese and tombs. A visit here provides not only spiritual insight but also an appreciation of the city's architectural and cultural heritage.

➢ Kraaling Park

Kraaling Park is a verdant oasis offering panoramic views of the Mediterranean and Antalya's dramatic cliffs. Its sprawling gardens, dotted with sculptures and shaded paths, are ideal for relaxing walks. Visitors can enjoy the park's cafes, children's play areas, and vibrant floral displays. A serene retreat within the city, it's perfect for unwinding or capturing stunning sunset photographs.

➢ Antalya Museum

Antalya Museum is a treasure trove of artifacts spanning the region's history, from prehistoric times to the Ottoman era. Its highlights include exquisite Roman sculptures, ancient mosaics, and a collection of Lycian relics. The museum's well-curated exhibits offer an in-depth understanding of Antalya's cultural evolution. Recognized as one of Turkey's top museums, it's a must-visit for history enthusiasts.

➢ Kaliese Marina

Kaliese Marina combines historic charm with modern leisure, offering a picturesque setting for boat tours and waterfront dining. Surrounded by cliffs and Ottoman-style architecture, the harbor is vibrant with activity. Visitors can admire luxury yachts, explore local shops, or enjoy fresh seafood at seaside restaurants. Whether day or night, the marina's lively atmosphere provides a memorable experience.

➢ Antalya Cable Car

The Antalya Cable Car ride to Timekeeper offers breathtaking views of the city, coastline, and Taurus Mountains. Ascending to an elevation of 605 meters, the journey is as stunning as the destination. At the summit, visitors can enjoy refreshments while soaking in panoramic vistas. Perfect for photographers and nature lovers, this experience showcases Antalya's beauty from a unique perspective.

Best Restaurants in Antalya

➢ Vanilla Restaurant

Vanilla Restaurant is renowned for its innovative approach to Turkish cuisine, blending traditional flavors with modern twists. Located by the sea, it offers stunning panoramic views of Antalya's coastline. The restaurant's sleek, contemporary interior complements the gourmet dishes served here. Known for its exceptional service and creative menu, Vanilla promises a fine dining experience that elevates the tastes of Turkey's diverse culinary heritage.

➢ Alp Pasa Restaurant

Alp Pasa Restaurant, set within a historic Ottoman mansion, offers a beautiful ambiance with a rich cultural atmosphere. The restaurant specializes in authentic Turkish cuisine, using fresh local ingredients to craft flavorful traditional dishes. Guests can dine in a charming courtyard surrounded by historic stone walls, making it an unforgettable setting. With its attentive service and refined menu, Alp Pasa offers a true taste of Turkish culinary tradition.

> ## 7 Mehmet

7 Mehmet is a chic and contemporary restaurant that combines local Turkish flavors with modern culinary techniques. Situated with a beautiful terrace offering spectacular views of the Mediterranean, this restaurant is a favorite for both locals and tourists. Known for its exquisite mezes, fresh seafood, and expertly grilled meats, 7 Mehmet creates a delightful dining experience in a stylish yet relaxed environment. It's perfect for those seeking a taste of Antalya's best traditional fare.

> ## Le Petit Chef

Le Petit Chef offers a one-of-a-kind dining experience with its 3D dinner show that combines culinary artistry with visual entertainment. As you dine, a miniature chef "appears" on your table, guiding you through a creative story of the meal. The menu is diverse, offering international and Mediterranean dishes with a modern presentation. Le Petit Chef is perfect for those looking for an immersive dining experience that engages all senses.

➢ Lathe Restaurant

Lathe Restaurant is a fine dining destination specializing in Mediterranean cuisine, with an emphasis on fresh, seasonal ingredients. The elegant atmosphere and exceptional service make it an ideal spot for special occasions. With a menu that combines the flavors of the Mediterranean with sophisticated presentations, Lathe delivers a memorable dining experience. Guests can enjoy beautifully prepared dishes like seafood, grilled meats, and seasonal vegetables in a relaxed yet refined setting.

➢ Felicita

Felicita is a beloved Italian restaurant in Antalya, renowned for its authentic pasta, wood-fired pizzas, and warm ambiance. Offering a cozy yet contemporary atmosphere, the restaurant captures the essence of traditional Italian cuisine with a modern touch. Whether you're craving a creamy pasta dish or a crispy pizza, Felicita delivers on flavor and quality. It's a great spot for families, couples, and anyone seeking a delicious Italian meal with a personal touch.

➢ Pastorale

Pastorale is an international restaurant that brings together an array of flavors from Turkish, Italian, and French cuisines. Set in a charming location, the restaurant offers a diverse menu that appeals to all palates. Whether you're in the mood for a hearty Turkish kebab, a light Italian pasta, or a classic French dish, Pastorale delivers exceptional food with flair. Its inviting atmosphere and varied options make it a fantastic choice for a versatile dining experience.

> ## ➢ Ayar Milanesi

Ayar Milanesi offers an authentic Turkish methane experience, known for its vibrant atmosphere and delicious meze platters. Serving a wide variety of cold and hot meze, as well as flavorful raki and other traditional drinks, this restaurant captures the essence of Turkish dining culture. Guests can enjoy the lively ambiance while sampling fresh seafood, grilled meats, and local specialties. It's the perfect place to experience traditional Turkish methane-style dining with friends and family.

> ## ➢ Searer

Searer is a popular restaurant that specializes in fresh, high-quality seafood and other local specialties. Known for its elegant setting and attentive service, Searer provides a refined dining experience in the heart of Antalya. The menu focuses on Mediterranean flavors, offering a variety of fresh fish, seafood platters, and seasonal vegetables. Whether enjoying a casual lunch or a romantic dinner, Searer's ambiance and culinary expertise make it a must-visit for seafood lovers.

> ## ➢ Terrace Steak House

Terrace Steak House is a top choice for steak lovers, offering a range of perfectly grilled cuts with a side of breathtaking sea views. The restaurant's modern decor and relaxed atmosphere provide the ideal setting for a memorable meal. With a menu that includes tender steaks, grilled vegetables, and flavorful sides, Terrace Steak House ensures that every bite is satisfying. It's an excellent choice for those seeking a delicious, high-quality steak while enjoying stunning panoramic views.

Best Shopping Centers in Antalya

➤ Antalya Miros Shopping Mall

Antalya Miros Shopping Mall is one of the largest and most popular shopping destinations in the city. It features a wide range of international and local stores, from fashion and electronics to home goods. The mall also has a variety of dining options, offering both casual eateries and upscale restaurants. With entertainment options such as a cinema and a children's play area, Antalya Miros provides a full shopping experience for families and tourists alike.

➤ Deepu Outlet Center

Deepu Outlet Center is a favorite for bargain hunters looking for high-quality products at discounted prices. Located just outside the city center, this outlet mall offers a range of designer brands, including clothing, accessories, and footwear. In addition to fashion outlets, it also has a variety of restaurants and cafes for visitors to relax and enjoy. Deepu is a great place to shop for those seeking luxury goods without the premium price tag.

➤ Mall of Antalya

Mall of Antalya is a modern and vibrant shopping center featuring a vast selection of stores, restaurants, and entertainment venues. It boasts an array of international brands, offering everything from clothing to electronics. The mall also features a large cinema, making it a perfect spot for a day of shopping and entertainment. With its sleek design and a variety of dining options, Mall of Antalya caters to all tastes and preferences.

➤ Veracity

Veracity is one of Antalya's most popular shopping malls, offering a mix of upscale and casual shopping experiences. The mall houses a variety of well-known brands, along with numerous restaurants and cafes for dining. Visitors can enjoy a cinema and ample parking space, making it a convenient destination for families and tourists.

Veracity provides an inviting environment for those seeking high-quality products and services in the heart of the city.

➤ Mark Antalya

Mark Antalya is a contemporary shopping center that offers a diverse range of retail stores, restaurants, and entertainment options. With its stylish design and strategic location in the city center, the mall attracts both locals and tourists. It features popular international and Turkish brands, and its food court offers a variety of culinary options. Mark Antalya also has a cinema, making it a complete shopping and entertainment hub for visitors of all ages.

➤ Agora Antalya

Agora Antalya is a large shopping mall offering a wide range of stores, restaurants, and entertainment options. The mall features both high-street fashion brands and more affordable options, making it a great destination for all types of shoppers. With its spacious design and modern architecture, Agora provides a comfortable environment for leisurely shopping. It also offers a cinema, making it a popular spot for entertainment after a day of shopping.

➤ Dilek Park

Dilek Park is a well-known shopping mall in Antalya, offering a variety of stores, restaurants, and family-friendly activities. In addition to fashion and home goods retailers, the mall includes a bowling alley, making it a great choice for entertainment. The food court offers a variety of local and international cuisine, catering to different tastes. Dilek Park is a convenient and fun place to shop, dine, and enjoy leisure activities for visitors of all ages.

➢ The Land of Legends

The Land of Legends is not only a theme park but also a shopping mall that offers an exciting blend of entertainment and retail experiences. Visitors can enjoy thrilling rides and shows, then shop at high-end boutiques and specialty stores. The mall features both international and Turkish brands, along with plenty of dining options. As one of the most unique shopping experiences in Antalya, The Land of Legends is perfect for those seeking both fun and shopping.

➢ Nova mall Manavgat

Nova mall Manavgat is located in the nearby town of Manavgat and provides a great shopping experience for those traveling outside Antalya. The mall features a wide variety of stores, including fashion, electronics, and home goods, catering to all types of shoppers. In addition, Nova mall offers a range of dining options and a comfortable environment for spending a relaxing day. It's a popular spot for both locals and tourists looking for quality shopping outside of the city center.

➢ Alkanium Center

Alkanium Center, located in Alanya, is a popular shopping mall offering a mix of fashion stores, restaurants, and entertainment options. The mall is home to a range of local and international brands, providing plenty of shopping choices. Visitors can enjoy the spacious food court or relax at one of the mall's cafes. Alkanium Center is an ideal shopping destination for those exploring Alanya, offering a variety of products and services for all ages.

➤ Time Center

Time Center, situated in Alanya, offers a diverse range of shopping opportunities with its variety of retail stores. From fashion and electronics to accessories and souvenirs, Time Center caters to both locals and tourists. The mall is known for its relaxed shopping atmosphere and convenient location. It also includes several restaurants and cafes, making it an ideal spot to shop, dine, and enjoy a leisurely day out in Alanya.

Nightlife in Antalya

Bars

➤ Filipa Café-Bar

Filipa Café-Bar is a lively and vibrant spot in Antalya, known for its welcoming ambiance and live music performances. This popular bar attracts both locals and tourists who come to enjoy its wide selection of drinks and the lively atmosphere. Whether you're looking to unwind with friends or dance along to the tunes of local musicians, Filipa provides a fun and energetic night out in the heart of the city.

➤ The Rock Bar

The Rock Bar is a haven for rock music lovers, offering a laid-back yet energetic atmosphere. Located in central Antalya, this bar plays classic rock, indie, and alternative tunes, making it the go-to spot for fans of live music. With its casual vibe, great drinks, and regular live performances, The Rock Bar is perfect for those looking to enjoy some good music and a relaxed night out.

➤ Odin Pub

Odin Pub is a classic Irish-style pub located in Antalya, offering a wide selection of beers, spirits, and cocktails. Known for its cozy atmosphere, Odin Pub is the ideal place to unwind after a day of sightseeing. Whether you're here for a casual pint with friends or looking to enjoy a night out, the bar's friendly vibe and variety of drinks ensure an enjoyable time for all visitors.

➢ Tipsy Old Town

Tipsy Old Town is a trendy bar located in the charming streets of Antalya's Old Town (Kaliese). With its stylish rooftop terrace, it offers stunning views of the city and the Mediterranean coastline. Guests can enjoy a refreshing cocktail or a chilled beer while soaking in the vibrant atmosphere. The laid-back ambiance, coupled with great music, makes it a popular spot for both locals and tourists looking for a memorable evening out.

➢ Grace Lounge Kalelike

Grace Lounge in Kalelike is a sophisticated lounge bar known for its intimate atmosphere and elegant setting. Offering an exceptional selection of fine wines, premium cocktails, and spirits, it caters to those with a refined taste. The chic décor, combined with mellow music, creates a perfect backdrop for a relaxing evening with friends or a romantic night out in the heart of Antalya's historic district.

Clubs

➢ Club Inferno

Club Inferno, located in Kemer near Antalya, is one of the city's most renowned nightclubs, known for its electrifying atmosphere and international DJs. The club regularly hosts high-energy parties, with cutting-edge light shows, great sound systems, and a mix of electronic and dance music. If you're looking for a night of dancing and excitement, Club Inferno offers an unforgettable experience for partygoers from around the world.

➢ Gaga Club Lara

Gaga Club in Lara is a vibrant nightlife venue offering a dynamic mix of electronic and house music. With its modern interior design and top-notch sound system, the club attracts both locals and tourists looking for a high-energy dance experience. The club often features performances by well-known DJs, making it one of the hottest spots for those who love electronic music and a lively party scene in Antalya.

➢ Havana Club

Havana Club brings the vibrant energy of Cuba to Antalya, offering a lively atmosphere filled with dancing, cocktails, and live music. The Cuban-themed nightclub features salsa and reggaeton music, allowing guests to dance the night away to tropical rhythms. Known for its fun vibe and tropical cocktails, Havana Club is a popular venue for those looking to enjoy a night of Cuban-inspired entertainment and culture.

➢ Club 29

Club 29 is one of Antalya's most stylish and modern nightclubs, offering a variety of music genres to suit all tastes. From electronic beats to classic hits, the club's diverse playlists keep the dance floor buzzing throughout the night. With its sleek interior, stunning light displays, and exclusive vibe, Club 29 offers an upscale nightclub experience perfect for those looking for an exciting and trendy venue in the heart of Antalya.

➢ Soho Bar Club Sensation

Soho Bar Club Sensation is a popular hotspot in Antalya's nightlife scene, known for its energetic atmosphere, music, and vibrant crowd. The club features a mix of music, ranging from popular dance tracks to electronic beats, ensuring everyone can enjoy the rhythm. Whether you're into dancing, enjoying a drink with friends, or soaking in the lively ambiance, Soho Bar Club Sensation offers a fantastic experience in the heart of the city.

You can also take a nice evening walk.

Exploring Antalya in 7 Days

Day 1: Arrival and Initial Exploration in Antalya

- **Morning:** Upon your arrival in Antalya, check into your hotel and take some time to unwind. Start your adventure with a delicious Turkish breakfast at a local café, where you can try classic items like simit (sesame-covered bread), mermen (scrambled eggs with tomatoes and peppers), and fresh olives. Enjoy the morning sun and get a feel for the city's vibrant atmosphere.

- **Afternoon:** Head to Antalya's Old Town (Kaliese) for your first exploration. Wander through its cobblestone streets lined with charming Ottoman houses, local shops, and cafes. Visit Hadrian's Gate, a grand Roman triumphal arch, and stroll along the picturesque harbor for beautiful views of the Mediterranean.
- **Evening:** For dinner, enjoy traditional Turkish meze and seafood at a waterfront restaurant in the Old Town. Afterward, take a peaceful evening walk along the marina, watching the sunset over the sea, and enjoy the tranquil surroundings.

Day 2: Beaches and Ancient Sites

- **Morning:** Begin your day with a relaxing visit to Konya alti Beach. Stretch out on the sandy shore, swim in the crystal-clear waters, or enjoy water sports like jet skiing or parasailing. The beach is perfect for unwinding and taking in the beautiful scenery of the Mediterranean coast.

- **Afternoon:** After a relaxing morning, take a short trip to the nearby ancient city of Perge. Explore the well-preserved ruins, including the impressive Roman theater, stadium, and ancient gates. Learn about the city's rich history as you stroll through the remnants of this once-thriving settlement.
- **Evening:** Head back to the city and enjoy a dinner at one of Antalya's renowned restaurants, such as 7 Mehmet, offering classic Turkish dishes with a view of the sea. Afterward, take a leisurely walk around Kraaling Park, where you can relax and enjoy panoramic views of the Mediterranean.

Day 3: Waterfalls and Adventure

- **Morning:** Visit the stunning Duden Waterfalls, located just outside of Antalya. Explore both the Upper and Lower Duden Waterfalls, where water cascades over cliffs into crystal-clear pools. Enjoy a scenic walk through the lush greenery that surrounds the falls.
- **Afternoon:** For an adventure-filled afternoon, head to Köprülü Canyon National Park. Whether you're into rafting, canyoning, or hiking, this park offers a variety of thrilling activities. Take a rafting tour down the river, navigating through the canyon's rugged landscape.
- **Evening:** Return to Antalya and dine at a restaurant offering Mediterranean cuisine, such as Lathe Restaurant.

Savor dishes made with fresh, local ingredients and enjoy the laid-back ambiance of the restaurant before heading back to your hotel for a restful night.

Day 4: Exploring Ancient Ruins

- **Morning:** Dedicate your morning to exploring Aspen Dos Ancient Theater, one of the best-preserved Roman theaters in the world. Admire the architecture and imagine the performances that once took place in this grand structure. The site also offers a glimpse into the grandeur of the Roman Empire.
- **Afternoon:** Continue your exploration with a visit to the ancient city of Side. Wander through the ruins of the Temple of Apollo and the Roman theater. Stroll along the beaches and enjoy a scenic lunch overlooking the Mediterranean Sea.
- **Evening:** Head back to Antalya and explore the nightlife by visiting Tipsy Old Town, a trendy bar with a rooftop terrace that offers stunning views of the city and the sea. Enjoy a refreshing cocktail while taking in the vibrant atmosphere of the Old Town.

Day 5: Cultural and Historical Insights

- **Morning:** Visit the Antalya Museum, where you can immerse yourself in the rich history of the region. The museum houses artifacts from the prehistoric, Hellenistic, and Roman periods, offering an in-depth look at Antalya's past. Don't miss the impressive statues and ancient pottery.

- **Afternoon:** After the museum, visit the Yilin Minaret Mosque, a significant landmark of Antalya. Admire its unique, fluted minaret, which is a distinct feature of Seljuk architecture. Explore the surrounding area and enjoy a peaceful moment at the mosque.
- **Evening:** Enjoy dinner at Felicita, an Italian restaurant in the city, offering a variety of delicious pasta and pizza. Afterward, relax at a local café or lounge with a Turkish coffee or tea.

Day 6: Relaxation and Shopping

- **Morning:** Take the morning to relax at Lara Beach, known for its long stretches of sand and calm waters. Enjoy a leisurely swim or simply soak up the sun. The beach is perfect for unwinding before heading into the city for some shopping.
- **Afternoon:** Visit one of the major shopping malls in Antalya, such as Veracity or Mark Antalya. Browse through a variety of international and local stores, from high-end fashion to Turkish handicrafts. Stop for a light snack at one of the food courts or cafés within the mall.
- **Evening:** For dinner, head to a local restaurant for Turkish barbecue or meze platters. Afterward, explore the nightlife at Searer, a popular restaurant offering fresh seafood and other local specialties.

Day 7: Panoramic Views and Farewell

- **Morning:** Take the Antalya Cable Car up to Timekeeper Hill for panoramic views of the city and the Mediterranean coastline. The cable car ride is a unique experience that offers stunning vistas as you ascend the mountain.
- **Afternoon:** Spend your last afternoon shopping or relaxing at one of Antalya's spas, where you can enjoy a traditional Turkish bath (hammam) to unwind after a week of exploration. Alternatively, visit the Land of Legends, a theme park and shopping complex with rides, shows, and shops for a final taste of Antalya's fun side.
- **Evening:** Conclude your Antalya adventure with a delicious farewell dinner at a local restaurant, such as Terrace Steak House, where you can enjoy a steak while watching the sunset over the Mediterranean. Reflect on the memories you've made during your time in this beautiful coastal city.

.....Enjoy Antalya.....

CHAPTER 5

IZMIR

"Izmir is not just a city; it's a feeling that blends history, culture, and the Aegean breeze into a unique experience."

As Turkey's third-largest city, Izmir is a captivating destination with its vibrant streets, historic landmarks, and stunning coastline. Known as the "Pearl of the Aegean," it offers a perfect harmony of modernity and tradition. From ancient ruins to lively bazaars and sun-kissed beaches, Izmir invites travelers to explore its charm and beauty.

Best Areas to Stay in Izmir

➤ Alsace

This vibrant district is Izmir's cultural heartbeat, attracting locals and travelers alike with its dynamic blend of modernity and tradition. Stroll along the waterfront promenades lined with trendy cafes and restaurants, offering a mix of global and Turkish flavors. Boutiques and artisan shops beckon shoppers, while the district's nightlife buzzes with energy. Alsace seamlessly combines seaside charm with city vibrancy, creating an unforgettable experience for visitors.

➤ Konak

Konak serves as the soul of Izmir, offering a window into its historical and cultural richness. The iconic Izmir Clock Tower stands proudly in Konak Square, a beloved symbol of the city. Wander through Emerald Bazaar, a maze of vibrant stalls selling everything from spices to handcrafted goods. The area is also home to museums and mosques, making it an essential stop for history enthusiasts and culture seekers.

➤ Karşıyaka

Nestled on the northern shore of the Gulf of Izmir, Karşıyaka offers a delightful escape from the city's hustle. Its lush waterfront parks are perfect for leisurely strolls, and the local markets are brimming with fresh produce and handmade goods. Visitors can enjoy a relaxing stay at boutique hotels, dine at cozy eateries, and mingle with warm-hearted locals. Karşıyaka captures the essence of authentic Turkish hospitality.

➢ Cosme

A jewel of Turkey's Aegean coast, Cosme is synonymous with sun-soaked beaches and upscale leisure. Its azure waters are perfect for swimming and thrilling water sports like windsurfing and kitesurfing. Beyond its beaches, Cosme boasts vibrant nightlife, luxury resorts, and historic sites, such as its ancient fortress. With its blend of relaxation and excitement, Cosme is a must-visit for anyone seeking a luxurious coastal getaway.

➢ Ural

Ural exudes rustic charm with its sprawling vineyards, scenic olive groves, and inviting artisanal markets. This serene town is a paradise for wine enthusiasts, offering tastings and tours at its boutique wineries. Wander through quaint villages, dine on fresh seafood at coastal restaurants, or simply soak in the peaceful ambiance. Ural is the ultimate destination for those craving a connection to nature and a slower pace of life.

➢ Belova

Belova is a haven for wellness and nature lovers, celebrated for its therapeutic thermal spas and stunning landscapes. Relax in the rejuvenating mineral waters, believed to possess healing properties, or take the cable car up Dede Mountain for panoramic views of Izmir. Belova also offers scenic hiking trails, ideal for outdoor adventurers. Whether seeking relaxation or exploration, Belova promises a refreshing experience.

➢ Seferi Hisar

Turkey's first "slow city," Seferi Hisar enchants visitors with its laid-back lifestyle and authentic charm. Stroll through its historic streets lined with stone houses, sample organic produce at local markets, and bask on its tranquil beaches. The area's natural beauty and unhurried pace invite travelers to unwind and embrace simplicity. Seferi Hisar is the perfect retreat for those looking to escape the chaos and immerse in serenity.

Best Hotels to Stay in Izmir
Luxury Hotels

➤ Swissotel Büyük Efes Izmir

Indulge in unmatched luxury at this iconic 5-star hotel overlooking the Aegean Sea. Its rooftop terrace offers breathtaking panoramic views, making it a favorite for leisure and business travelers alike. Guests can unwind in its world-class spa, take a dip in multiple swimming pools, or savor gourmet cuisine at its exceptional restaurants. The hotel's elegantly designed rooms provide the ultimate blend of comfort and style.

➤ Izmir Marriott Hotel

Located in the vibrant heart of Konak, the Izmir Marriott Hotel redefines urban luxury. Its elegant rooms and suites come with stunning views, while the rooftop bar serves as a chic spot to enjoy the cityscape. Guests can rejuvenate at the spa, maintain their routine at the state-of-the-art fitness center, or explore nearby attractions. Its central location makes it an ideal base for both relaxation and exploration

➢ Wyndham Grand Izmir Odile Thermal & Spa

Combining luxury and wellness, this 5-star hotel is a haven for those seeking relaxation. It features thermal springs and a luxurious spa, providing a tranquil escape from the bustling city. Guests can also enjoy multiple pools, a fitness center, and elegantly furnished rooms with top-notch amenities. The hotel's commitment to comfort and well-being makes it a standout choice for travelers looking to recharge.

Mid-Range Hotels

➢ Renaissance Izmir Hotel

Situated in Konak, this stylish hotel offers both comfort and convenience. Its spacious rooms are designed with contemporary flair, while the rooftop bar provides breathtaking city views. Guests can dine at the hotel's delightful restaurant or unwind in the pool after a day of sightseeing. Its location within walking distance of many attractions ensures an unforgettable stay in Izmir without breaking the bank.

➢ Hilton Garden Inn Izmir Bairiki

Perfect for both business and leisure travelers, this modern hotel offers spacious rooms equipped with all the comforts you need. Guests can enjoy a refreshing dip in the indoor pool, keep fit at the gym, or savor international flavors at the on-site restaurant. Located in the bustling Bairiki area, it provides excellent accessibility to the city's key attractions and commercial hubs.

➤ Best Western Premier Karşıyaka Convention & Spa Hotel

Located in the charming Karşıyaka district, this hotel offers a perfect blend of leisure and convenience. Its comfortable rooms are complemented by a relaxing spa, an indoor pool, and a well-equipped fitness center. With easy access to the beach and city center, guests can enjoy the best of Izmir. The hotel's modern amenities and exceptional service make it a favorite among travelers.

Budget-Friendly Hotels

➤ Tavi Airport Hotel Izmir

A practical choice for travelers on the go, this hotel is conveniently located near Izmir International Airport. It offers cozy rooms with essential amenities, making it ideal for short stays or layovers. Guests can dine at the on-site restaurant or take advantage of the airport shuttle service. Despite its budget-friendly rates, the hotel ensures a comfortable and stress-free experience.

➤ Olympiad Hotel Izmir

Located in the heart of the city, this affordable hotel offers excellent value for money. It's simple yet cozy rooms provide a restful retreat after a day of exploration. Guests can enjoy meals at the in-house restaurant or relax on the rooftop terrace, which boasts beautiful views of the city. Its central location allows easy access to Izmir's top attractions and vibrant nightlife.

➤ The New Hotel Zeybek

This modern and stylish hotel in the Konak district is perfect for budget-conscious travelers. The comfortable rooms are designed to ensure a pleasant stay, while the on-site restaurant and bar provide convenient dining options. Its proximity to popular landmarks and public transport makes it an excellent base for exploring Izmir without sacrificing comfort or affordability.

Historical Sites

➤ Ephesus

Step into the ancient world at Ephesus, a UNESCO World Heritage Site renowned for its well-preserved ruins. Marvel at the grandeur of the Library of Celsus, wander through the awe-inspiring Great Theatre, and explore the remnants of the Temple of Artemis, one of the Seven Wonders of the Ancient World. A visit here offers a deep dive into the rich history and architectural brilliance of classical antiquity.

➤ Pergamon Acropolis

A historical gem located about 100 kilometers from Izmir, Pergamon is a UNESCO World Heritage Site that captivates visitors with its dramatic hillside ruins. Explore the steep terraces of the acropolis, stand in awe of the Great Altar of Zeus, and visit the renowned Library of Pergamon. The site's striking architecture and breathtaking views transport you back to its time of ancient prominence.

➢ Izmir Agora

Nestled in the heart of the city, Izmir Agora offers a glimpse into Roman life through its remarkably preserved ruins. Stroll through the colonnaded galleries, imagine the hustle and bustle of the ancient marketplace, and admire the intricate carvings that tell tales of a bygone era. This historical site connects visitors to Izmir's deep-rooted past amidst a modern urban setting.

Cultural Attractions

➢ Emerald Bazaar

Immerse yourself in the vibrant energy of Emerald Bazaar, a sprawling market where tradition and modernity meet. Discover colorful stalls offering spices, handmade jewelry, and Turkish textiles, or savor authentic street food as you wander through the narrow alleys. This lively bazaar is a must-visit for those looking to experience Izmir's culture and find unique treasures to take home.

➢ Konak Square

The beating heart of Izmir, Konak Square, is a historic and cultural centerpiece. Admire the iconic Izmir Clock Tower, a symbol of the city, and visit nearby landmarks like the Hisar Mosque and Yale Mosque. The square's dynamic atmosphere, surrounded by cafes and street performers, makes it an ideal spot to soak in the local culture and enjoy the lively city vibe.

➢ Kordon

This scenic waterfront promenade is a favorite among locals and visitors alike. Take a leisurely stroll along the coastline, watch the stunning Aegean sunset, or relax at one of the many cafes and restaurants offering sea views. Whether your people-watching, cycling, or simply enjoying the serene ambiance, Kordon captures the charm of Izmir's laid-back lifestyle.

Natural Beauty

➢ Cosme

A coastal paradise, Cosme is famous for its pristine beaches, turquoise waters, and vibrant nightlife. Spend your day lounging on golden sands, indulge in water sports like windsurfing or sailing, and explore the charming old town with its quaint streets and cafes. By night, the town comes alive with trendy bars and clubs, making it a perfect destination for relaxation and entertainment.

➢ Ural

A tranquil escape, Ural enchants visitors with its lush vineyards, olive groves, and coastal beauty. Tour the local wineries for tastings, explore the charming villages, and savor delicious dishes prepared with fresh, local ingredients. With its stunning views and slower pace of life, Ural offers a delightful mix of culinary experiences and natural serenity.

➢ Seferi Hisar

Turkey's first "slow city," Seferi Hisar, is a haven of peace and authenticity. Wander through its picturesque old town, unwind on its serene beaches, and enjoy the unhurried pace of life. Known for its commitment to sustainability and tradition, this charming town provides the perfect backdrop for a relaxing getaway steeped in natural beauty and cultural richness.

➢ Izmir Museum of History and Art

Uncover Izmir's fascinating past at this comprehensive museum featuring artifacts from the Bronze Age to the Ottoman era. Wander through its galleries showcasing ancient sculptures, ceramics, and jewelry that reflect the region's rich cultural heritage. The museum offers a captivating journey through time, perfect for history enthusiasts and curious travelers alike.

➢ Asansol

Take a ride on the historic Asansol elevator, built in 1907, and enjoy panoramic views of Izmir from its top. Originally constructed to help residents navigate the city's steep terrain, it now serves as a charming attraction with a rooftop cafe. The breathtaking vistas of the Aegean and the city make it a must-visit for photographers and sightseers.

➤ Izmir Wildlife Park

An adventure for nature and animal lovers, Izmir Wildlife Park offers a home to diverse species from around the globe. From majestic lions and playful monkeys to exotic birds and reptiles, the park provides a family-friendly experience. With its spacious enclosures and educational exhibits, it's a wonderful spot to connect with wildlife and learn about conservation efforts.

Best Restaurants in Izmir

➤ Deniz Restaurant

Deniz Restaurant offers an unforgettable dining experience with its wide selection of fresh seafood, including grilled fish, octopus, and squid. Set against a backdrop of stunning sea views, this iconic spot is a must-visit for seafood lovers. The combination of delectable dishes and picturesque scenery makes it a perfect place for a leisurely meal while enjoying the soothing sounds of the sea.

➤ Balıkçı Hasan

Balıkçı Hasan is a beloved local eatery known for its simple yet mouthwatering grilled fish. The focus here is on high-quality, fresh seafood, ensuring every dish is flavorful and satisfying. With a relaxed atmosphere and friendly service, it has become a favorite among residents and tourists alike. For an authentic, no-frills seafood experience, this spot is highly recommended.

➤ Tavai Recep Usta

Tavai Recep Usta is a culinary destination for those craving perfectly grilled meats, especially lamb and chicken. This renowned restaurant serves dishes cooked to perfection over an open flame, ensuring smoky, rich flavors in every bite. The emphasis is on traditional methods and top-quality ingredients, making it a prime choice for anyone seeking an authentic Turkish grilling experience.

➤ Floral Restaurant

Floral Restaurant offers a warm, welcoming atmosphere where guests can indulge in a wide array of traditional Turkish dishes.

From savory kebabs and hearty stews to fresh vegetables and flavorful mezes, this restaurant has something for everyone. Known for its attention to quality and authentic flavors, Floral is the perfect place to enjoy the best of Turkish home-cooked meals.

➢ Isabel Bagai

Isabel Bagai stands out as a historic restaurant that elevates traditional Turkish cuisine with a refined dining experience. Set in an elegant, timeless atmosphere, it offers an exquisite selection of grilled meats, mezes, and regional specialties. Perfect for those looking to savor both classic and contemporary Turkish dishes, this restaurant is a true gem in Izmir's culinary scene.

➢ La Kigali

For an elegant and sophisticated dining experience, La Kigali offers a delightful taste of French cuisine in Izmir. Known for its classic French dishes, such as croissants, escargots, and rich sauces, this restaurant delivers both in flavor and ambiance. Whether you're enjoying a romantic dinner or a special celebration, La Kigali offers a perfect escape into the world of French gastronomy.

➢ Ristorante Pizzeria Venetic

Ristorante Pizzeria Venetic brings the authentic flavors of Italy to Izmir with its delectable pizzas and pastas. Whether you're craving a classic Margherita or a hearty Bolognese, this Italian restaurant caters to all tastes. The cozy, inviting atmosphere and high-quality ingredients make it a popular spot for both casual diners and lovers of Italian cuisine.

➢ Alsace Dostaler Farini

Alsace Dostaler Farini is a bustling bakery known for its freshly baked bread, pastries, and savory börek. Whether you're stopping by for a quick breakfast or a satisfying snack, the variety and quality of offerings make it a local favorite. The cozy, inviting space makes it easy to grab a bite and enjoy a moment of respite amid the hustle of the city.

➢ Ayşa Boşnak Brackish

Ayşa Boşnak Brackish specializes in the iconic Turkish börek, offering flaky, golden pastries filled with a variety of delicious ingredients, including cheese, meat, and spinach. The perfect quick bite for those seeking authentic Turkish flavors, this bakery provides a taste of tradition with every pastry. Ideal for a light snack or a hearty meal, it's a must-try for pastry lovers.

Izmir's culinary scene is constantly evolving, offering new dining experiences that blend local flavors with international influences. Be sure to explore the diverse options, from fresh seafood to authentic Turkish dishes, and from quick bites to elegant international cuisine, as the city's vibrant food culture continues to surprise and delight visitors. Always check reviews and recommendations to stay up-to-date with the latest trends.

Modern Malls

➢ Forum Born ova

Forum Born ova is one of the largest shopping malls in Izmir, offering a wide selection of both international and local brands. With a spacious food court, a cinema, and even a bowling alley, it's not just a place to shop but a full entertainment destination. Whether you're looking for fashion, gadgets, or a fun day out with friends or family, Forum Born ova is the place to be.

➢ İzmir Optimum

İzmir Optimum combines shopping with leisure in a modern and spacious setting. Featuring a range of shops, from fashion boutiques to electronic stores, the mall also boasts a variety of restaurants, a cinema, and a children's play area. Whether you're shopping for the latest trends, enjoying a movie, or letting the kids play, it's a perfect spot for the whole family.

➢ MaviBahçe

MaviBahçe is a lively shopping center known for its vibrant atmosphere and diverse shopping options. Visitors can enjoy a mix of local and international brands, along with a wide range of restaurants and cafes in the food court. The mall also has a cinema, making it a perfect spot for both shopping and entertainment. With its lively vibe, MaviBahçe is a popular destination for all ages.

➢ Konak Pier

Konak Pier offers a luxurious shopping experience along the waterfront with beautiful sea views. Featuring high-end international brands, this shopping mall combines fashion with leisure. You can enjoy a relaxing stroll along the pier, indulge in gourmet dining, or shop for premium products. The stunning location and upscale offerings make Konak Pier a must-visit for those seeking a sophisticated retail experience.

➤ Ago/ran Shopping Center

Agora Shopping Center is an upscale mall with a curated selection of luxury brands, making it a top choice for fashion lovers. It also features a gourmet food court with a variety of fine dining options. The mall's elegant atmosphere and high-quality offerings ensure a premium shopping experience. Whether you're looking for high-end fashion or a gourmet meal, Agora delivers both in style.

Traditional Markets

➤ Emerald Bazaar

Emerald Bazaar is a historic marketplace that encapsulates the vibrant culture of Izmir. Winding through narrow streets, this bustling market offers everything from colorful spices and textiles to intricate Turkish handicrafts. It's the perfect place to immerse yourself in the local culture, haggle for unique finds, and experience the timeless charm of one of Izmir's oldest districts. A must-visit for lovers of authentic Turkish souvenirs.

➤ Alsace

Alsace is a trendy district known for its boutique shops and vintage stores, making it a favorite among fashion-forward locals and tourists. The streets are lined with eclectic shops offering unique clothing, accessories, and local art. The district's artistic atmosphere adds to its charm, and it's an excellent place to discover one-of-a-kind items. Alsace is perfect for a leisurely stroll and discovering hidden gems.

➤ Bastani

Bastani, located along Izmir's coast, is a bustling district with a wide variety of shops. From trendy clothing stores to home goods and accessories, you'll find plenty to explore. With its charming coastal vibe, Bastani offers a laid-back shopping experience. It's a great spot to pick up unique finds while enjoying the breeze from the sea, making it a perfect place to spend a day shopping and relaxing.

Best Places to visit in Izmir

Izmir, often called the "Pearl of the Aegean," is a city that seamlessly combines history, culture, and modernity. Known for its vibrant coastal vibe, Izmir offers an array of attractions that cater to every kind of traveler. Whether you're a history enthusiast, a nature lover, or a foodie, Izmir has something special to offer. Below are some of the must-visit places in Izmir:

➤ Konak Square and the Clock Tower

At the heart of Izmir lies Konak Square, a bustling area that reflects the city's dynamic spirit. The iconic Clock Tower, built in 1901, is the square's centerpiece and a symbol of the city.

Surrounded by vibrant markets, cafés, and historic buildings, this is the perfect place to start your Izmir exploration

➤ Kemeralti Bazaar

Immerse yourself in the lively atmosphere of Kemeralti Bazaar, one of the oldest and most traditional markets in Turkey. Wander through its labyrinthine alleys, brimming with shops selling everything from textiles and jewelry to spices and souvenirs. It's also a fantastic spot to try authentic Turkish street food like boyoz and kumru.

➤ Alsancak

Alsancak is a chic district renowned for its lively nightlife, boutique shops, and waterfront promenades. The area's trendy cafés, restaurants, and bars attract locals and visitors alike. Take a leisurely walk along Kordon, a scenic promenade with stunning views of the Aegean Sea.

➤ Ephesus (Day Trip)

Just a short drive from Izmir, Ephesus is a historical treasure
trove. This ancient city, once a thriving hub of Greek and Roman
civilizations, is home to remarkable landmarks like the Library of
Celsus, the Great Theatre, and the Temple of Artemis.

➤ Kadifekale (Velvet Castle)

Perched atop a hill, Kadifekale offers panoramic views of Izmir
and the surrounding bay. This ancient fortress, built during
Alexander the Great's reign, is steeped in history and provides an
excellent opportunity for sightseeing and photography.

➤ Agora Open-Air Museum

Dive into Izmir's ancient past at the Agora Open-Air Museum.
This well-preserved Roman marketplace features arches,
columns, and inscriptions that transport visitors back to the city's
early days. It's a must-visit for history buffs.

➤ Cesme and Alacati (Day Trip)

For a more relaxed vibe, head to the charming towns of Cesme
and Alacati. Cesme is famous for its pristine beaches and thermal
springs, while Alacati is known for its cobblestone streets,
windsurfing spots, and stunning boutique hotels.

➤ zmir Archaeological Museum

This museum houses an impressive collection of artifacts from
ancient Greek, Roman, and Byzantine periods. From intricate

statues to ancient pottery, the exhibits provide a fascinating glimpse into the region's rich history.

➤ Izmir Wildlife Park

A wonderful spot for families, Izmir Wildlife Park is a vast natural habitat where you can see a variety of animals up close. The park is eco-friendly and offers a peaceful escape from the city.

Seferihisar (Turkey's First Cittaslow)

Seferihisar is a charming town known for its slow-paced life and focus on sustainable living. Stroll through its peaceful streets, enjoy fresh organic produce, and unwind in this idyllic setting that has earned its title as Turkey's first "Citta slow" (slow city).

Nightlife In Izmir

➤ Alsace Bars and Clubs

Alsace is the heart of Izmir's nightlife, buzzing with trendy bars, clubs, and lounges. Gazi Kadina Socage is a hotspot for music lovers, offering venues with live performances and DJ sets. Sardinia Café & Bar is popular for its live jazz, while Varuna Gezgin Café combines international cuisine with themed nights. The district promises a lively atmosphere for locals and tourists to unwind and enjoy.

➤ Konak's Nightlife

Konak offers a mix of historic charm and vibrant nightlife, catering to a diverse crowd. Sayanora Nightclub stands out with its stylish ambiance and renowned international DJs. Vecchi Bar is perfect for those seeking classic cocktails in an elegant setting. Broadway Night Club provides a lively space for dancing and live music. With its variety, Konak ensures an unforgettable night out in Izmir.

> ## Karishama's Laid-back Vibes

For a more relaxed evening, head to Karishama, known for its cozy bars and waterfront pubs. Enjoy a drink by the sea or explore the district's quieter venues that offer an intimate setting. It's a great place to socialize with locals, indulge in craft beers, or savor traditional mezes paired with Turkish raki. Karishama is perfect for those who prefer a calm yet enjoyable nightlife experience.

> ## Esme's Beach Clubs

A short drive from Izmir, Cosme is renowned for its energetic beachside nightlife. Clubs like Sole Mare and Paparazzi offer late-night dancing, live performances, and a stunning seaside backdrop. Spend the evening sipping cocktails on the sand or dancing under the stars. Esme's lively scene attracts a mix of locals and international visitors, making it a must-visit for those seeking vibrant nightlife near Izmir.

➤ Kordon Promenade

Kordon Promenade is a picturesque spot for evening relaxation, featuring a range of cafes, wine bars, and restaurants. Stroll along the waterfront while enjoying the sea breeze and the city lights. It's an ideal place for a casual drink, romantic date, or simply soaking in the lively atmosphere. The area's mix of laid-back and chic venues makes it a versatile option for nightlife enthusiasts

➤ Born ova's Student Hotspots

Home to several universities, born ova have a youthful vibe and an array of affordable nightlife options. The district features student-friendly bars, pubs, and live music venues that cater to a younger crowd. Explore local favorites for cheap drinks, upbeat music, and energetic crowds. With its vibrant energy and eclectic scene, born ova offer a dynamic and fun-filled nightlife experience in Izmir.

➤ Live Music at Hayal Kovesi Izmir

Hayal Kovesi is a popular venue for live music, hosting local and international bands in an intimate setting. Located in Alsace, it's a favorite among music lovers looking to enjoy rock, jazz, or indie performances. The venue offers a lively yet cozy atmosphere, making it perfect for those who appreciate great tunes paired with delicious drinks and snacks.

➤ Jazz and Blues at 1888

1888 is a must-visit for jazz and blues enthusiasts, offering live performances in a charming setting. Located in Alsace, this bar combines a vintage ambiance with top-notch acoustics, creating an unforgettable musical experience. Enjoy expertly crafted cocktails while listening to talented local and international artists. It's an excellent choice for those seeking a sophisticated and soulful night out in Izmir.

➤ Rooftop Bars in Izmir

For breathtaking views of the city and Aegean Sea, rooftop bars like Sky Bar at Swissotel and La Vie Nouvelle are perfect choices. These venues combine panoramic vistas with premium drinks, creating a chic nightlife experience. Whether you're sipping cocktails at sunset or enjoying a late-night gathering under the stars, rooftop bars in Izmir offer a stylish way to end your day.

➤ Izmir Night Markets

For a unique nighttime experience, explore Izmir's vibrant night markets. These lively bazaars offer everything from street food and handcrafted souvenirs to live entertainment. The bustling atmosphere, combined with local delicacies and music, provides an authentic taste of Turkish culture. Night markets are an excellent option for those who want to enjoy the city's lively spirit without heading to traditional bars or clubs.

CHAPTER 6

CAPPADOCIA

"Cappadocia is where dreams meet reality—stay in its heart and wake up to a world shaped by time, history, and nature."

Cappadocia, a land of fairy chimneys and cave hotels, offers diverse options for every traveler. Each area has its unique charm, from bustling hubs to serene retreats, ensuring an unforgettable stay.

Best Areas to Stay in Cappadocia

➤ Goree

Goree is the heart of Cappadocia, renowned for its proximity to must-see attractions like the Goree Open-Air Museum and hot air balloon launch sites. The town is filled with charming cave hotels, cozy restaurants, and lively markets. It's an excellent choice for first-time visitors, adventurers, and anyone who wants to be at the center of the action

➤ Akhisar

Set atop a hill, Akhisar boasts breathtaking views of the valleys, especially from the iconic Akhisar Castle. This area is ideal for travelers seeking tranquility, upscale cave hotels, and a luxurious ambiance. Stroll through its picturesque streets, enjoy local fine dining, and take in the serene atmosphere. Akhisar is perfect for a romantic or high-end getaway.

➤ Urge

Urge is a hub for elegance, offering luxurious cave hotels, wine-tasting experiences, and gourmet dining options. Known for its sophisticated vibe, it's a favorite for couples and honeymooners. Explore local vineyards, relax in stylish accommodations, or visit nearby attractions like Three Beauties. Urge combines charm and convenience for those seeking a refined Cappadocian retreat.

➤ Avanos

Avanos, situated along the Kyzylorda River, is famous for its pottery workshops and artisan community. The town offers a peaceful ambiance with boutique hotels and cafes overlooking the river. Travelers can participate in pottery-making or explore its charming streets. It's an excellent base for art enthusiasts and those looking to unwind near Cappadocia's cultural heart.

➢ Cauvin

This quaint village, nestled among ancient rock formations, offers a quiet, historical escape. Cauvin is home to ancient churches, like St. John the Baptist Church, and rustic accommodations. Ideal for travelers seeking solitude, it's a great starting point for hiking adventures in the surrounding valleys. Cauvin provides a mix of history, nature, and a peaceful atmosphere.

➢ Orta Hisar

Orta Hisar, with its towering rock castle and traditional Turkish vibe, is a cultural gem in Cappadocia. The area features charming boutique hotels, local eateries, and a warm community feel. Travelers can explore nearby attractions like Pincerlike Valley or immerse themselves in the area's history. It's an excellent choice for cultural enthusiasts and those wanting a blend of tradition and comfort.

➢ Mustafa Pasa

Mustafa Pasa, a beautifully preserved Greek village, is a haven of architectural beauty and serene charm. Its cobblestone streets, historic buildings, and boutique hotels make it ideal for those seeking a unique cultural experience. Visitors can enjoy peaceful walks, local delicacies, and the area's calm atmosphere. Mustafa Pasa is perfect for travelers looking to escape the crowds and soak in Cappadocia's heritage.

Luxury Hotels and Resorts in Turkey

For an indulgent stay, Cappadocia offers luxurious cave hotels and world-class resorts. Properties like the Museum Hotel in Akhisar provide top-tier services, infinity pools overlooking the valleys, and gourmet dining. These hotels combine modern amenities with traditional charm, ensuring a unique experience. Ideal for honeymooners and high-end travelers, these luxury stays redefine comfort amidst Cappadocia's magical landscapes.

Boutique Hotels and Traditional Stays

Boutique hotels in Cappadocia blend tradition and comfort, offering personalized services in intimate settings. These charming accommodations, often carved into caves or historic buildings, provide a unique stay steeped in history. Enjoy local touches like handmade decor and regional breakfasts. Perfect for cultural enthusiasts, boutique stays offer an authentic and cozy way to experience Cappadocia's magic.

Budget-Friendly Accommodation Options

Travelers on a budget can find excellent accommodations throughout Cappadocia without sacrificing comfort. Guesthouses and smaller cave hotels in areas like Goree and Orta Hisar offer affordable rates, warm hospitality, and easy access to major attractions. Many budget options include traditional Turkish breakfasts and local guidance for exploring the region. These stays are ideal for backpackers and adventurers seeking value for money.

Best Hotels in Cappadocia

➤ Luxury Cave Hotels

Museum Hotel: A masterpiece of luxury and history, the Museum Hotel is set within a 10th-century cave complex. Each room is uniquely designed with antique furnishings, offering an immersive experience. Guests can enjoy an outdoor infinity pool overlooking the valley, a world-class spa, and fine dining with locally sourced ingredients. Its panoramic terrace is ideal for sunrise views, especially during the hot air balloon flights.

Argos in Cappadocia: Nestled in a meticulously restored historical cave complex, Argos in Cappadocia blends luxury with authenticity. Its elegant rooms and suites feature private terraces and unique touches like fireplaces and wine taps. The hotel's sprawling grounds include vineyards and lush gardens, providing breathtaking views of the valleys. Argos offers an unparalleled dining experience at Seki Restaurant, known for its fusion of local and international cuisines.

Kayak Api Premium Caves: This luxurious retreat is located in the historical Kayak Api neighborhood, offering a blend of tradition and modernity. The spacious cave rooms are equipped with state-of-the-art amenities, including heated floors and rain showers. Guests can savor local flavors at the on-site restaurant or relax on the rooftop terrace, offering sweeping views of the Cappadocian landscape. The hotel also features a Turkish bath and wellness center.

➢ Mid-Range Cave Hotels

Divan Cave House: Divan Cave House combines affordability with comfort and charm. The hotel features cozy rooms with authentic cave interiors and modern touches. Its on-site restaurant serves delicious Turkish cuisine, while the rooftop terrace offers panoramic views of Goree and the surrounding valleys. Guests can enjoy guided tours and balloon ride bookings directly through the hotel.

Cappadocia Cave Suites: A perfect blend of history and comfort, Cappadocia Cave Suites offers a variety of room options, including private plunge pool suites. The hotel is located near Goree Open-Air Museum, making it a convenient base for exploration. Guests can enjoy hearty breakfasts on the terrace while marveling at the hot air balloons. Its friendly staff and thoughtful amenities ensure a memorable stay.

Kelebek Special Cave Hotel & Spa: Known for its warm hospitality, Kelebek offers a range of accommodations, from traditional cave rooms to luxurious suites. Guests can indulge in spa treatments, traditional Turkish baths, and organic meals at the restaurant. The rooftop terrace provides spectacular views of the Goree valleys, particularly enchanting during sunrise and sunset.

➤ Budget-Friendly Cave Hotels

Cappadocia Caves Hotel: This budget-friendly option provides clean and comfortable cave rooms with traditional decor. Guests can enjoy a simple yet authentic experience in a central location. The hotel offers a complimentary breakfast and is within walking distance of Goree's attractions and dining options, making it an excellent choice for travelers on a budget.

Arif Cave Hotel: Arif Cave Hotel stands out for its welcoming atmosphere and incredible value. Situated at the top of a hill, it boasts stunning panoramic views of the Goree landscape. The rooms are simple but cozy, and the friendly staff is always ready to assist with local recommendations and tours. It's a perfect choice for backpackers or families.

Goree Cave Lodge: This lodge offers affordable accommodations without compromising on charm. Its cave rooms are well-maintained, and some even come with small private balconies. The communal terrace is a favorite among guests for its sunrise views. The hotel is known for its delicious homemade breakfasts and easy access to nearby hiking trails.

➤ Important Considerations

Location: Proximity to attractions such as Goree Open-Air Museum, Akhisar Castle, and the valleys is essential. Goree is ideal for first-time visitors, while Akhisar and Urge cater to those seeking serenity and luxury.

Amenities: Check for added features like spas, pools, terraces, or private tours. Mid-range and luxury hotels often offer guided activities, adding convenience to your stay.

Price: While luxury hotels provide unparalleled comfort, budget-friendly options also offer a cozy and authentic Cappadocian experience. Select one based on your preferences and travel goals.

Booking in Advance: Secure your accommodation well ahead of time, especially during peak seasons (spring and autumn) when Cappadocia experiences high tourist influx.

Best Place to Stay in Cappadocia

➤ Goree

Pros: Goree is the heart of Cappadocia, offering a vibrant atmosphere with a wide range of accommodations, from luxury cave hotels to budget-friendly lodges. It provides easy access to top attractions like the Goree Open-Air Museum and hot air balloon rides. The town is filled with cafes, shops, and tour operators, making it perfect for first-time visitors and adventurers seeking convenience.

Cons: As the most popular area, Goree can get crowded, especially during peak tourist seasons like spring and autumn. The bustling streets and influx of visitors may detract from the serene experience that many travelers seek in Cappadocia. Prices for accommodations and dining can also be higher compared to less central areas.

> ➢ **Unhair**

Pros: Perched on a hilltop, Akhisar boasts breathtaking panoramic views of Cappadocia's valleys and iconic rock formations. The tranquil atmosphere is perfect for families or travelers seeking an upscale and quieter experience. Akhisar Castle is a must-visit landmark, offering spectacular sunset and sunrise views. It's an ideal spot for those who love photography and serenity.

Cons: While Akhisar offers a peaceful retreat, it has fewer dining and shopping options compared to Goree. Travelers looking for a more bustling social scene or diverse restaurant choices may find it limiting. It's also less convenient for accessing some of the region's major attractions without transportation.

➢ Urge

Pros: Urge offers an authentic Turkish experience with a rich history and a focus on wine culture and traditional cuisine. The area is known for its elegant cave hotels, providing luxurious stays at more affordable prices than Goree. It's a fantastic destination for food lovers, with plenty of fine dining options and opportunities to sample Cappadocian wines.

Cons: Being less centrally located, Urge requires more travel time to reach key attractions. The lack of nearby sights within walking distance might make it less appealing for those relying on public transportation or preferring a more compact itinerary.

➢ Orta Hisar

Pros: Orta Hisar is known for its peaceful and authentic atmosphere, making it a great choice for travelers looking to escape the crowds. Its affordable accommodations and charming boutique hotels provide a cozy retreat. The impressive Orta Hisar Castle offers a glimpse into the region's history and stunning views of the surrounding landscape.

Cons: The town has limited dining and shopping options compared to Goree or Urge. Its less central location might pose challenges for visitors without private transportation, as accessing attractions and amenities requires some planning.

➤ Cauvin

Pros: A small, historic village, Cauvin offers a quiet and serene environment ideal for travelers seeking solitude. Its stunning views of ancient rock-cut churches and unique landscapes make it a photographer's dream. Affordable accommodation options and a laid-back vibe attract those wanting a more relaxed experience.

Cons: Similar to Orta Hisar, Cauvin has fewer dining and shopping options, which may require guests to venture to nearby towns for meals or supplies. Its less central location means accessing popular attractions may take more time, making it less convenient for some travelers.

Sayah Han Restaurant

Sayah Han offers an authentic Turkish dining experience in a cozy, cave-style setting. Known for its rich mezes, slow-cooked lamb dishes, and fresh breads, the restaurant caters to both locals and tourists. Its scenic terrace provides stunning views of Cappadocia's valleys, making it a perfect spot for a memorable meal. The warm hospitality and traditional ambiance elevate the experience further.

Best Restaurants in Cappadocia

> ### Seten Anatolian Cuisine

Seten is a must-visit for those seeking traditional Cappadocian and Anatolian dishes. Specialties include pottery kebabs and stuffed grape leaves, served with locally sourced ingredients. Its charming rooftop terrace offers panoramic views of Goree's unique landscapes. The restaurant's cozy atmosphere, coupled with attentive service, makes it a favorite for romantic dinners and group gatherings alike

> ### Ziggy's Café & Restaurant

Located in Urge, Ziggy's is famed for its creative take on Turkish cuisine, offering a mix of traditional and modern flavors. Signature dishes include slow-cooked lamb shanks and spiced auberge. The eclectic interior, adorned with local handicrafts, creates a welcoming and artistic vibe. Guests also appreciate the rooftop terrace, which provides breathtaking views of the surrounding hills.

➢ Old Cappadocia Café & Restaurant

Situated in the heart of Goree, Old Cappadocia Café delivers a mix of Turkish and international flavors. Popular menu items include their grilled meats, fresh salads, and vegetarian-friendly options. The friendly staff and rustic décor add charm to this casual eatery. The outdoor seating area offers a relaxing spot to enjoy delicious food while soaking in Cappadocia's magical atmosphere.

➢ Aravan Evi Restaurant

Nestled in the quaint village of Avail, Aravan Evi focuses on organic, farm-to-table dining. The family-run establishment serves traditional Turkish dishes made with fresh ingredients from their own farm. Guests rave about their homemade yogurt, bulgur pilaf, and clay pot casseroles. With its tranquil setting and warm hospitality, it's an ideal choice for a quiet, authentic meal.

➢ Dibek Restaurant

Dibek is a cozy, family-run restaurant located in Goree, renowned for its authentic pottery kebabs and traditional Turkish dishes. Meals are served in a rustic, cave-like setting, with low tables and floor seating for a traditional experience. The extensive menu also features vegetarian options. With its friendly service and home-cooked flavors, Dibek offers an unforgettable taste of Cappadocia.

➢ Lila Restaurant

Housed in the luxurious Museum Hotel, Lila is an upscale dining option for those seeking gourmet Turkish and international cuisine. Each dish is crafted with finesse, using local and seasonal ingredients. The restaurant's elegant ambiance and spectacular views of Cappadocia's valleys make it ideal for special occasions. The extensive wine list features selections from Turkey's best vineyards

➢ Top deck Cave Restaurant

This intimate, cave-style restaurant in Goree is celebrated for its small menu of freshly prepared Turkish specialties. Favorites include stuffed eggplants, lamb stew, and homemade desserts. The cozy setting, with just a few tables, ensures a personalized experience. Top deck is popular among travelers seeking authentic flavors and a warm, family-run atmosphere.

➢ Inci Cave Restaurant

Inci Cave Restaurant blends traditional Turkish flavors with modern presentations in a cave-inspired dining room. Their highlight dishes include chicken with apricots and beef with figs, showcasing unique flavor combinations. The elegant ambiance is complemented by attentive service, making it a great choice for a special dinner. Guests often enjoy their meal with a glass of Cappadocian wine.

➢ Pumpkin Goree Restaurant and Art Gallery

Pumpkin Goree combines delicious Turkish cuisine with an artistic flair. The limited menu focuses on fresh, locally sourced ingredients, featuring dishes like lamb chops, grilled vegetables, and baklava. The charming courtyard is filled with art and local crafts, creating a vibrant dining environment. Its intimate setting and creative vibe make it a standout choice in Goree.

Best Places to visit in Cappadocia

➢ Goree Open-Air Museum

A UNESCO World Heritage Site, the Goree Open-Air Museum is a fascinating collection of rock-hewn churches and monasteries adorned with vivid frescoes. It offers a glimpse into the region's Christian history and the monastic life of early inhabitants. The stunning art, intricate carvings, and serene surroundings make it a must-visit destination. Don't miss the Dark Church for its remarkably preserved frescoes.

➢ Akhisar Castle

Akhisar Castle is a towering rock formation offering panoramic views of Cappadocia's iconic landscapes. This ancient fortress, carved into the natural rock, served as a strategic lookout point in history. Visitors can climb to the top to witness breathtaking vistas of fairy chimneys, valleys, and distant mountains. It's an ideal spot for photography and a serene place to catch the sunset.

➢ Daikyu Underground City

Daikyu is one of Cappadocia's largest underground cities, a marvel of ancient engineering. This subterranean wonder was used as a refuge during invasions, with interconnected tunnels spanning multiple levels. Visitors can explore its living quarters, chapels, kitchens, and even stables. The intricate design and historical significance make it a captivating experience for history and architecture enthusiasts.

➢ Pasa bag (Monks Valley)

Pasa bag, also known as Monks Valley, is famous for its surreal fairy chimneys, some of which have dual or triple caps. These unique formations were once inhabited by hermit monks, adding a spiritual dimension to the site. Stroll through the valley to admire the natural wonders and learn about the fascinating geology that shaped them. It's a perfect spot for photography and quiet reflection.

➢ Love Valley

Named for its phallic-shaped rock formations, Love Valley is a stunning natural site showcasing Cappadocia's geological beauty. Visitors can hike through the valley, surrounded by towering pillars and lush vegetation. The scenic trails offer breathtaking views and opportunities to connect with nature. It's a romantic spot, often frequented by couples, and a favorite for witnessing magical sunrises.

➢ Avanos and Kyzylorda River

Avanos is a charming town known for its pottery-making traditions and the picturesque Kyzylorda River. Stroll through its cobbled streets to explore artisan workshops and participate in pottery-making classes. The riverbank offers a tranquil setting for a leisurely walk or a riverside café experience. The blend of artistic heritage and natural beauty makes Avanos a unique and memorable destination.

➢ Red Valley (Kicukiro)

Red Valley is renowned for its striking red-hued rock formations, particularly stunning during sunrise and sunset. The valley offers scenic hiking trails that wind through hidden churches, caves, and lush vineyards. Its serene ambiance makes it a favorite for nature lovers and photographers. The glowing red tones of the rocks create a magical atmosphere, perfect for an unforgettable Cappadocian adventure.

➢ Devran Valley (Imagination Valley)

Devran Valley, also called Imagination Valley, is famous for its whimsical rock formations resembling animals and objects. Visitors can let their imagination run wild, spotting formations shaped like camels, seals, and more. Unlike other valleys, it has no caves or churches, making it unique in its artistic appeal. It's a great place for families, offering fun photo opportunities and a playful vibe

➢ Ihlara Valley

Ihlara Valley is a lush canyon with a winding river and towering cliffs, offering a refreshing escape in Cappadocia. It's dotted with ancient rock-cut churches and frescoes, making it a mix of natural beauty and historical intrigue. The valley's hiking trails lead visitors through serene landscapes and charming villages. It's an excellent spot for a peaceful day of exploration and relaxation.

➢ Goree Panorama Viewpoint

Goree Panorama Viewpoint provides one of the most iconic views of Cappadocia, with sweeping vistas of fairy chimneys and rugged landscapes. It's an ideal spot to start or end your day, offering incredible photo opportunities and a serene ambiance. During sunrise, the sky fills with colorful hot air balloons, creating a magical scene. It's a must-visit for capturing Cappadocia's breathtaking beauty.

Nightlife in Cappadocia

➢ Red Wine House

Red Wine House in Urge is a cozy spot for wine enthusiasts, offering an extensive selection of Cappadocia's finest wines. The intimate setting, adorned with rustic decor, is perfect for unwinding after a day of exploring. Guests can enjoy live jazz or acoustic performances, adding a touch of elegance to the evening. The knowledgeable staff enhances the experience with personalized recommendations.

➢ Angel Café Bistro Bar

Located in Goree, Angel Café Bistro Bar is a lively venue for cocktails and music. The vibrant atmosphere attracts locals and tourists alike, offering a mix of upbeat tunes and stunning rooftop views. Their signature cocktails and local wines pair well with delicious appetizers. It's a great place to socialize or relax while soaking in the beauty of Cappadocia at night.

➢ Fat Boys Bar

A popular hangout spot in Goree, Fat Boys Bar combines a laid-back vibe with lively entertainment. Known for its friendly staff and reasonably priced drinks, it's a go-to for travelers seeking a casual night out. Enjoy pool tables, darts, and a mix of international and local tunes. The outdoor seating adds to the charm, making it ideal for warm Cappadocian nights.

➢ One Way Café & Bar

Situated in Avanos, One Way Café & Bar offers a bohemian atmosphere perfect for relaxing evenings. Guests can enjoy handcrafted cocktails, Turkish wines, and a variety of snacks. The eclectic music selection sets the tone, ranging from mellow jazz to upbeat classics. With its riverside location and artistic interior, this bar is a unique nightlife experience in Cappadocia.

➢ Turkuaz Balloons Wine House

For a truly unique nightlife experience, Turkuaz Balloons Wine House offers wine tasting with a view of Cappadocia's iconic hot air balloons. Located in Akhisar, it provides a serene and romantic setting. Savor local wines while gazing at the illuminated valleys below. This spot is perfect for couples or those seeking a peaceful yet memorable evening.

➢ Hebei Restaurant & Bar

Hebei is a lively venue in Urge that transforms into a buzzing bar at night. Known for its vibrant live music scene, it showcases local and international artists. The menu features a range of drinks and late-night snacks. The mix of great music, friendly crowds, and a welcoming atmosphere makes it a top choice for nightlife in Cappadocia.

➢ Old Cappadocia Bar

This charming bar in Goree combines history with a modern twist, set in a restored cave. It offers a wide range of wines, beers, and cocktails, with friendly bartenders ready to craft your drink of choice. The cozy interiors and occasional live music create a relaxed yet lively vibe. It's a favorite spot for mingling with fellow travelers or enjoying a quiet drink.

➢ Restaurant & Lounge

No:10 is a sophisticated lounge in Akhisar that offers a refined nightlife experience. Sip on expertly crafted cocktails or Cappadocian wines while enjoying breathtaking views of the fairy chimneys. The stylish décor and intimate lighting create a chic ambiance, perfect for unwinding after a day of sightseeing. Occasional live music adds to its allure.

➤ Mahen Sarpa Evi (Wine House)

Mahen Sarpa Evi in Avanos is a hidden gem for wine lovers. This quaint wine house specializes in locally produced wines, offering tastings and pairings. The dimly lit, cave-like interiors provide a cozy and romantic atmosphere. Friendly staff are happy to guide guests through Cappadocia's rich wine culture, making it a perfect spot for a laid-back evening.

➤ Retro Cappadocia Bar

Retro Cappadocia Bar in Goree lives up to its name with its vintage-inspired décor and eclectic music playlist. From retro classics to Turkish hits, the vibe is both nostalgic and fun. Guests enjoy a wide selection of beverages, from craft beers to creative cocktails. The warm and inviting atmosphere ensures a memorable evening, whether you're dancing or simply relaxing with friends.

CHAPTER 7
MUSEUMS, HISTORY, AND HIDDEN GEMS IN TURKEY

"Turkey is a living museum, where ancient history whispers through every stone and hidden gems await discovery. From world-renowned sites to secret beaches and tranquil villages, every corner offers a new chapter in the story of this magical land."

Turkey's rich cultural and historical heritage is reflected in its diverse museums, ancient sites, and hidden treasures. From the bustling metropolis of Istanbul to the quiet villages of the Aegean coast, Turkey offers a plethora of experiences for those interested in delving into its fascinating history. Museums, historical ruins, and off-the-beaten-path destinations provide visitors with unique insights into the country's past and natural beauty.

➢ Top Museums in Istanbul, Ankara, and Ephesus

Istanbul, Turkey's cultural hub, is home to an impressive array of museums that showcase the country's rich past. The Tokai Palace Museum is a must-see, offering a glimpse into the opulence of the

Ottoman Empire. Located in the heart of Istanbul, the palace was the seat of Ottoman sultans for centuries and now displays artifacts, manuscripts, and treasures that provide insight into the empire's history. Nearby, the Hagia Sophia Museum is a blend of Byzantine and Ottoman influences, a former church and mosque now standing as a museum with stunning mosaics and architectural beauty. Also not to be missed is the Istanbul Archaeological Museum, where ancient sculptures, pottery, and treasures from Greece, Rome, and the Middle East are displayed.

Moving to the capital city of Ankara, the Ankara Museum of Anatolian Civilizations is a treasure trove of historical artifacts from ancient Anatolian civilizations. The museum's impressive collection includes Hittite, Phrygian, and Urartian artifacts, including the famous King Midas' golden burial treasures. For a deeper understanding of Turkish culture and history, the Atatürk Mausoleum (Antilabor) in Ankara is an iconic site that commemorates Mustafa Kemal Atatürk, the founder of the Turkish Republic.

In Ephesus, the Ephesus Archaeological Museum provides a fascinating insight into the ancient city, one of the most well-preserved Greco-Roman cities in the world. Visitors can marvel at the artifacts from the Temple of Artemis, one of the Seven Wonders of the Ancient World, and the ruins of the ancient library. The museum's collection includes sculptures, inscriptions, and everyday items that offer a glimpse into life in one of the ancient world's most important cities.

➤ Exploring Turkey's Historical Sites: Troy, Pergamon, and Beyond

Turkey is home to some of the most significant archaeological sites in the world, including Troy, Pergamon, and other ancient ruins that narrate the country's rich history. Troy, immortalized by Homer's epic Iliad, was once a bustling city-state during the late Bronze Age. Visitors can explore the ancient ruins, including the famed Troy Walls, the City Gates, and the reconstructed Troy VI houses. The site offers a unique opportunity to walk through history, surrounded by remnants of ancient walls and temples that have sparked fascination for centuries.

Pergamon, located in modern-day Bergama, is another UNESCO World Heritage site. The Acropolis of Pergamon features monumental ruins, including the Altar of Zeus, a grand structure that once hosted elaborate rituals. The Pergamon Museum, situated at the site, is known for its stunning reconstructions of these artifacts and sculptures, including the Athena Temple and the Library of Pergamon, one of the largest in the ancient world. The ruins of Asclepius, an ancient medical center dedicated to the Greek god of healing, are another highlight, showcasing the importance of Pergamon as a center for medicine and knowledge.

Further south, the ruins of Aspen Dos, home to one of the best-preserved Roman theaters, are a testament to the grandeur of Roman architecture. The Aphrodisiac site, with its impressive Temple of Aphrodite, also stands out for its stunning sculptures and ancient ruins. Turkey's ancient cities, from Miletus to Hierapolis, offer a diverse range of historical sites that highlight the country's role as a bridge between the East and West, both culturally and geographically.

➤ Hidden Gems: Secret Beaches, Villages, and Nature Spots

While Turkey is famous for its major tourist destinations, it also hides numerous gems that remain relatively unknown to the masses. The Aegean and Mediterranean coastlines are dotted with secluded beaches that offer tranquility and natural beauty. Butterfly Valley, near Fisheye, is one such secret paradise, accessible only by boat or a challenging hike, with crystal-clear waters and a stunning backdrop of cliffs. The valley is also home to the rare Jersey Tiger Butterfly, adding to its charm.

The Data Peninsula is another hidden gem, known for its pristine beaches and picturesque villages. The small towns like Palamutbükü offer a peaceful escape from the crowds, with traditional stone houses, quiet beaches, and clear waters perfect for swimming and sailing. Bozcaada, an island off the coast of

Kankakee, is another peaceful retreat known for its vineyards, untouched beaches, and charming, whitewashed homes.

For nature lovers, the Kakkar Mountains in northeastern Turkey is a paradise. The region is known for its lush green landscapes, alpine lakes, and rugged peaks, offering excellent hiking and trekking opportunities. Similarly, Ihlara Valley, with its lush environment, cave dwellings, and rock-hewn churches, is a tranquil retreat offering a combination of natural beauty and historical significance. These hidden gems are often less crowded and offer visitors the chance to experience Turkey's authentic beauty away from the bustling tourist hotspots.

CHAPTER 8
MUST TRY DISHES IN TURKEY

"Turkey's flavors tell a story—rich, bold, and unforgettable.".

➢ Döner Kebab: Succulent, Slow-Roasted Meat

Döner Kebab is one of Turkey's most iconic dishes, celebrated worldwide for its tender, flavorful meat. Thinly sliced lamb, chicken, or beef is slow-roasted on a vertical rotisserie, allowing the juices to caramelize the meat to perfection. Typically served in warm pita bread or lavash wrap, it's often accompanied by fresh vegetables, tangy sauces, and a sprinkle of sumac. Alternatively, it can be presented on a plate alongside rice and salad, making it a versatile meal. The succulent taste of döner, combined with the crunch of fresh greens and the richness of sauces, creates an irresistible culinary experience. Whether grabbed on the go from street vendors or savored in a restaurant, döner kebab is a must-try for any visitor to Turkey.

➢ Adana Kebab: Spicy, Grilled Minced Meat Skewers

Named after the city of Adana, Adana Kebab is a fiery, flavorful delight for spice lovers. Made from minced lamb or beef, the meat is blended with red pepper flakes, garlic, and spices before being shaped onto flat metal skewers. The kebabs are then grilled over an open flame, imparting a smoky, charred flavor that pairs perfectly with the bold spices. Served with flatbread, grilled vegetables, and a side of fresh herbs or rice, Adana Kebab is as visually appealing as it is delicious. The rich aroma of sizzling meat wafting through the air is a common and mouthwatering experience in Turkey's street markets and restaurants alike.

➤ İskender Kebab: A Feast of Flavors on a Plate

İskender Kebab is a luxurious version of the classic döner, named after its creator from Bursa, İskender Efendi. Tender slices of lamb or beef are arranged over a bed of diced pita bread, then drenched in a rich tomato sauce. The dish is finished with a generous dollop of yogurt on the side and a drizzle of sizzling butter poured over the top. This layering of flavors creates a symphony of textures—crispy bread softened by the sauce, the juicy meat, and the cool, tangy yogurt. Every bite delivers a balanced blend of savory, tangy, and buttery flavors that make İskender Kebab an unforgettable culinary experience

➢ Kebab: Grilled Meat Skewers with a Side of Tradition

Kebabs are a staple in Turkish cuisine, offering endless variations that highlight the region's rich culinary heritage. Whether made from lamb, beef, chicken, or even fish, the meat is typically marinated in a blend of olive oil, garlic, and spices before being grilled to perfection. Served with fluffy rice, grilled vegetables, or fresh salad, kebabs are a favorite at family gatherings and festive occasions. Each region in Turkey has its own unique twist on the classic kebab, making it a diverse and delicious dish worth exploring multiple times during any trip.

➢ Manti: Tiny Dumplings Packed with Flavor

Manti are small dumplings filled with minced meat or spiced vegetables, often referred to as "Turkish ravioli." These delicate pockets of flavor are boiled or steamed and then served with a generous helping of garlicky yogurt and a drizzle of melted butter infused with red pepper flakes. Each bite-sized piece offers a delightful combination of soft dumpling, savory filling, and creamy sauce. Manti are labor-intensive to make, often reserved for special occasions, but their rich, comforting taste makes them a treasured dish in Turkish homes and restaurants.

➢ Dolma: Stuffed Vegetables Bursting with Flavor

Dolma, meaning "stuffed" in Turkish, is a beloved dish made from vegetables such as bell peppers, grape leaves, or zucchini, filled with a mixture of rice, herbs, pine nuts, and sometimes minced meat. The filling is infused with olive oil, dill, and lemon juice, creating a fresh, tangy flavor. Whether served warm or cold, dolma is a staple of Turkish mezze (small plates) and are a perfect balance of light and satisfying. The blend of textures—from the soft, tender vegetables to the flavorful filling—makes dolma a delightful addition to any meal.

➤ Pied: Turkey's Unique Take on Pizza

Pied, often referred to as "Turkish pizza," is a boat-shaped flatbread topped with a variety of ingredients, making it a beloved comfort food across Turkey. The dough is handmade and baked in a traditional stone oven, resulting in a crispy, golden crust. Common toppings include minced meat, cheese, spinach, or sukuk

(Turkish sausage), and a perfectly cooked egg can be added to the center for an extra indulgent touch. Served hot and sliced into pieces, pied is best enjoyed with a side of salad or Aryan, a refreshing yogurt drink. Whether in a bustling restaurant or a local bakery, biting into the soft, savory bread layered with fresh ingredients is an unforgettable experience.

➢ Lahman: Thin, Crispy, and Packed with Flavor

Lahman is a thin, round flatbread topped with a spicy mixture of minced meat, tomatoes, onions, and a blend of herbs and spices, often referred to as Turkish flatbread pizza. Unlike pied, it's rolled out flat and baked to a crispy perfection. Lahman is typically served with a side of fresh parsley, lemon wedges, and sometimes sliced onions. Diners roll it up with the fresh ingredients, squeeze a bit of lemon juice on top, and enjoy it like a wrap. Light, crispy, and bursting with flavor, Lahman is a popular street food and a quick, satisfying meal for locals and tourists alike

➢ Kofta: Flavorful Turkish Meatballs

Kofta, or Turkish meatballs, are a versatile and popular dish, made from ground lamb or beef mixed with breadcrumbs, onions, garlic, and a blend of spices like cumin and paprika. These flavorful meatballs can be grilled, fried, or baked and are often served with rice, salad, or flatbread. There are many regional variations of kofta, such as Ingol Kofta and Akwaaba Kofta, each offering a unique twist. Whether enjoyed at a roadside stand or a fine dining restaurant, kofta's juicy, spiced meat makes it a comforting and delicious meal that embodies the essence of Turkish home cooking.

➤ Mene men: A Turkish Breakfast Classic

Mene men is a traditional Turkish breakfast dish consisting of scrambled eggs cooked with tomatoes, green peppers, onions, and spices. It's typically prepared in a small, shallow pan and served with crusty bread for dipping. Mene men's rich, savory flavor is enhanced with the addition of Turkish chili flakes or feta cheese for those who like an extra kick. Often shared among friends and family, Mene men is more than just a dish—it's a symbol of Turkish hospitality and togetherness, making it a beloved breakfast option that's simple yet satisfy.

➤ Baklava: A Sweet, Nutty Delight

Baklava is Turkey's most famous dessert, made from layers of thin, flaky pastry filled with chopped nuts—usually pistachios or walnuts—and soaked in a fragrant syrup of honey or sugar with a hint of rosewater or orange blossom. Each bite of baklava delivers a satisfying crunch followed by the rich, sweet filling that melts in your mouth. Typically enjoyed with a cup of Turkish tea or coffee, baklava is a treat that symbolizes celebration and indulgence. Found in bakeries and cafes across Turkey, it's the perfect way to end a meal or enjoy a sweet afternoon snack

➤ Kunefe: A Unique Blend of Sweet and Savory

Kunefe is a crispy, sweet pastry filled with melted cheese and soaked in syrup, offering a unique balance of savory and sweet flavors. Made from shredded phyllo dough called kadaifi, it's baked until golden and crispy, then doused in a sugar syrup and topped with crushed pistachios. Served hot, kunefe is gooey on the inside and crunchy on the outside, making it an irresistible dessert. Often enjoyed in the evening, kunefe is a rich and decadent way to conclude a meal.

➢ Lokum: The Sweet World of Turkish Delight

Lokum, known internationally as Turkish Delight, is a soft, chewy confection made from sugar, starch, and flavorings such as rosewater, lemon, or pomegranate. Often dusted with powdered sugar or coconut flakes, locum comes in a variety of flavors and sometimes contains nuts like pistachios or hazelnuts. Each piece is a small bite of sweetness that's perfect for savoring slowly. It's commonly offered as a gesture of hospitality, making it a cherished part of Turkish culture and a delightful souvenir for visitors.

➢ Simit: Turkey's Iconic Street Snack

Simit, often called the Turkish bagel, is a ring-shaped bread encrusted with sesame seeds. Crispy on the outside and soft on the inside, simit is a quintessential street food found on every corner of Turkey. Vendors push carts loaded with fresh simit through bustling streets, offering it as a quick and affordable snack. Traditionally served plain, it pairs perfectly with cheese, olives, or a cup of Turkish tea. Simit is not only a popular breakfast item but also a beloved symbol of Turkish street culture, providing a delicious, portable bite for locals and tourists alike.

➢ Börek: Flaky Pastry with Savory Fillings

Börek is a traditional Turkish pastry made from thin layers of dough called Yuka, filled with savory ingredients such as cheese, spinach, or minced meat. Baked or fried to golden perfection, börek comes in various shapes—spirals, rolls, or large trays sliced into squares. It's a staple at Turkish breakfast tables and tea times, known for its rich, buttery layers and satisfying fillings. The crispy exterior and soft, flavorful center make börek a versatile dish that's both hearty and comforting, perfect for any time of day.

➢ Çay: The Heart of Turkish Hospitality

Çay, or Turkish tea, is more than a beverage—it's a cherished ritual and symbol of hospitality. Brewed strong and served in small tulip-shaped glasses, it's typically enjoyed without milk, allowing the robust flavor to shine. Çay is offered in every home, shop, and café, often accompanied by sweets like locum or simit. Whether sipped during a business meeting or a friendly gathering, Turkish tea fosters conversation and connection, embodying the warmth of Turkish culture.

➢ Kahne: The Rich Tradition of Turkish Coffee

Turkish coffee, or cave, is an iconic part of Turkey's cultural heritage, known for its bold flavor and unique brewing method. Made by finely grinding coffee beans and boiling them with water and sugar in a special pot called a cezve, it's served unfiltered in small cups, leaving a thick layer of grounds at the bottom. Often accompanied by a piece of Turkish delight, cave is more than a drink—it's an experience, traditionally followed by fortune-telling from the remaining coffee grounds, adding a touch of mystique to this rich, aromatic beverage

➢ Aryan: A Refreshing Yogurt Drink

Aryan is a cool, tangy yogurt-based drink that's both refreshing and nutritious. Made by mixing yogurt, water, and a pinch of salt, it's the perfect accompaniment to spicy Turkish dishes like kebabs or Lahman. Aryan is served chilled, often frothy, and provides a soothing contrast to the heat of Turkish cuisine. Widely consumed across Turkey, Aryan is a favorite during the hot summer months, offering a refreshing alternative to sugary sodas and a healthy way to stay hydrated.

➢ Mercie Cobras: Hearty Lentil Soup

Mercie Cobras, or lentil soup, is a staple of Turkish home cooking, known for its simplicity and comforting taste. Made from red lentils, onions, carrots, and a blend of spices like cumin and paprika, it's pureed into a smooth, velvety consistency. Often garnished with a squeeze of lemon and served with crusty bread, this soup is a popular starter at Turkish meals and a go-to comfort food during colder months.

➢ Ili Kofta: A Crispy Delights with a Spicy Filling

Ili Kofta, or stuffed meatballs, are a delectable Turkish delicacy made from a crispy bulgur shell filled with a mixture of ground meat, walnuts, onions, and aromatic spices. Shaped like an oval and deep-fried to a golden brown, isle kofta has a crunchy exterior that gives way to a juicy, flavorful center. It's often served as an appetizer or snack, offering a satisfying combination of textures and a rich, savory taste.

CHAPTER 9

Travel Tips for Exploring Turkey

"A healthy traveler is a happy traveler. Drink plenty of water, eat local, and take care of your body to fully embrace the wonders Turkey has to offer."

Turkey offers a wealth of experiences, from its bustling cities to its tranquil beaches and ancient ruins. To make the most of your trip while keeping costs low and ensuring a safe and healthy journey, here are some essential travel tips.

➤ Budget Travel Tips: Exploring Turkey Affordably

Traveling Turkey on a budget is entirely possible with a few smart strategies. opt for public transportation like buses, trams, and domus (shared minivans), which are both efficient and economical. Street food is not only affordable but delicious, offering treats like simit, börek, and döner kebabs for a fraction of the cost of sit-down meals. Look for guesthouses or boutique hostels in areas like Goree or Izmir for charming yet affordable accommodations. Booking domestic flights in advance can also help save on travel between cities, as Turkey's budget airlines often have promotions. Lastly, consider visiting during the shoulder seasons (spring or fall) when prices are lower, and crowds are fewer.

➤ Safety Tips for Visitors: Staying Secure in Turkey

Turkey is generally a safe destination, but like any travel, taking precautions is essential. Keep your belongings close, especially in crowded markets and tourist hotspots, to avoid pickpocketing. Use reputable transportation services, especially at night, and avoid unlicensed taxis. It's wise to respect local customs and dress modestly, particularly when visiting mosques or rural areas. Registering your travel plans with your country's embassy and keeping emergency contacts handy adds an extra layer of security. Stay updated on local news and government travel advisories for any potential risks during your visit.

➢ Health and Wellness Tips: Staying Healthy While Traveling

Maintaining your health while traveling in Turkey is essential to enjoy the experience fully. Stay hydrated, especially in summer, and always drink bottled water. Turkish cuisine is diverse and delicious, but if you have dietary restrictions or allergies, communicate them clearly to avoid issues. Carry a basic travel health kit with medications for common ailments like digestive issues or headaches. Take advantage of Turkey's thermal spas, such as those in Pamuk kale or Belova, for relaxation and wellness. Lastly, wear sunscreen and comfortable shoes, as you'll likely be doing plenty of walking under the sun.

➢ Cultural Etiquette Tips: Respecting Local Traditions

Understanding Turkey's cultural norms will enhance your travel experience. When visiting mosques, dress modestly and remove your shoes before entering. Public displays of affection are generally frowned upon, especially in more conservative areas. Always greet locals with a polite "Marhaba" (hello) or "Tasker Ede rim" (thank you). Haggling is expected in markets but should be done respectfully. Lastly, it's customary to offer or accept tea during conversations, as it is a sign of hospitality

➢ Packing Tips: What to Bring for a Turkish Adventure

Packing for Turkey requires a balance of comfort and practicality. Bring lightweight clothing for summer and layers for cooler months, especially if visiting regions like Cappadocia or Eastern Turkey. Comfortable walking shoes are a must for exploring historical sites and cobblestone streets. Include a scarf for visiting religious sites, and don't forget essentials like sunscreen, a reusable water bottle, and a power adapter for European outlets. A Turkish phrasebook can also be helpful.

➤ Best Times to Visit Turkey: Seasonal Tips for Travelers

The best time to visit Turkey depends on what you want to experience. Spring (April to June) and autumn (September to November) offer mild weather, perfect for exploring Istanbul, Ephesus, and Cappadocia. Summer is ideal for coastal destinations like Bodrum and Antalya but can be hot in inland areas. Winter provides a unique opportunity to see Cappadocia's fairy chimneys dusted with snow and enjoy the ski resorts of Mount Uludağ.

➤ Must-Try Experiences: Making the Most of Your Trip

Maximize your Turkish adventure with unforgettable experiences. Take a hot air balloon ride over Cappadocia at sunrise for breathtaking views. Explore the bustling Grand Bazaar in Istanbul for unique souvenirs. Visit Pamuk kale's travertine terraces for a natural spa experience. Don't miss a traditional hammam (Turkish bath) for relaxation, and savor local delicacies like baklava, Turkish delight, and freshly brewed Turkish coffee to immerse yourself in the flavors of the country.

CHAPTER 10
10 DAYS ITINERARY IN TURKEY

"Discover Turkey in 10 days: a perfect blend of history, culture, and breathtaking landscapes."

➤ Day 1: Arrival in Istanbul

Your adventure begins as you arrive in Istanbul, Turkey's vibrant metropolis where East meets West. After settling into your hotel, take a leisurely evening stroll along the Bosphorus or through the historic Sultanahmet district, where you can admire the iconic Blue Mosque and Hagia Sophia under the evening sky. Enjoy a traditional Turkish dinner, perhaps in one of the city's rooftop restaurants overlooking the Bosphorus Strait. This day serves as a perfect introduction to Istanbul's blend of history, culture, and modern flair.

➤ Day 2: Explore Istanbul's Historic Sites

Dedicate your second day to exploring the historical heart of Istanbul. Start with a visit to the Hagia Sophia, a stunning fusion of Byzantine and Ottoman architecture, before heading to the Tokai Palace, home to sultans and their treasures. Afterward, visit the Blue Mosque, one of the most recognized landmarks in Istanbul. Don't miss the Basilica Cistern, an underground marvel that will transport you back in time. Finish your day at the Grand Bazaar, where you can shop for unique souvenirs.

➤ Day 3: Day Trip to the Princes' Islands

On Day 3, take a ferry ride to the Princes' Islands, an idyllic retreat just off the coast of Istanbul. The largest, Bayada, offers an escape from the bustling city, with picturesque views, quaint streets, and historic mansions. The islands are car-free, so cycling or horse-drawn carriage rides are popular ways to explore. Enjoy fresh seafood at a seaside restaurant before returning to Istanbul for the night.

➤ Day 4: Travel to Cappadocia

On Day 4, travel to Cappadocia, a region famous for its surreal landscapes and unique cave dwellings. Upon arrival, check into one of the region's famous cave hotels for a one-of-a-kind experience. Spend the evening marveling at the region's natural beauty, with its unique fairy chimneys and valleys illuminated by the setting sun.

➢ Day 5: Hot Air Balloon Ride and Goree Open-Air Museum

Start your day early with a hot air balloon ride over the incredible landscapes of Cappadocia. As the sun rises, you'll float above the famous fairy chimneys and cave dwellings. Afterward, head to the Goree Open-Air Museum, a UNESCO World Heritage site, to explore its rock-cut churches and Byzantine frescoes. You'll spend the rest of the day hiking through the stunning valleys, including Pasa bag Valley, home to remarkable mushroom-shaped formations.

➢ Day 6: Explore Avanos and Kayali Underground City

On Day 6, visit the charming town of Avanos, known for its pottery workshops. Try your hand at pottery-making before exploring the ancient Kayali Underground City, a maze of subterranean tunnels and rooms used as refuges by early Christians. You can spend the evening enjoying a delicious Turkish dinner and watch a Whirling Dervishes performance, a mesmerizing cultural experience.

➢ Day 7: Travel to Pamuk kale

Next, travel to Pamuk kale, renowned for its otherworldly white travertine terraces formed by mineral-rich hot springs. Take a dip in the warm waters and enjoy the therapeutic effects while soaking in the panoramic views of the surrounding valley. Visit the ancient Roman city of Hierapolis, which sits atop the terraces, and explore the ruins of its well-preserved amphitheater and Roman baths.

➢ Day 8: Explore Ephesus

From Pamuk kale, head to the ancient city of Ephesus, one of the best-preserved archaeological sites in the world. Walk through the ancient streets of this Greco-Roman city and visit the remarkable Library of Celsus, the Temple of Artemis, and the Great Theatre. The ruins of Ephesus will transport you back in time, offering a glimpse of what life was like in one of the most important cities of the ancient world.

➢ Day 9: Visit Izmir and Travel to Antalya

On Day 9, travel to Izmir, a coastal city known for its vibrant markets and lively culture. Stroll through Konak Square, visit the ancient Agora, and sample local dishes in the city's renowned restaurants. In the afternoon, continue your journey south to Antalya, a beautiful city located on the Mediterranean coast, known for its stunning beaches and rich Roman history. Spend your evening by the Mediterranean, soaking in the picturesque views.

➢ Day 10: Relax in Antalya

Your last day in Turkey is dedicated to relaxation. Spend the morning exploring Antalya's Old Town (Kaliese), where narrow, cobblestone streets lead to charming boutiques, cafes, and Roman-era landmarks like Hadrian's Gate. In the afternoon, unwind on one of Antalya's beaches or visit the Duden Waterfalls, located just outside the city. Your trip ends with a memorable sunset over the Mediterranean before you head to the airport for your flight home.

CHAPTER 11

FACTS ABOUT TURKEY

"Turkey is a land where ancient history, vibrant culture, and breathtaking landscapes come together, offering a unique experience at every turn."

Turkey is a fascinating country that bridges Europe and Asia, offering a unique blend of cultures, history, and landscapes. Its official name is the Republic of Turkey, and it spans across both continents with the majority of its territory located in Asia. The country is home to approximately 84 million people, making it one of the most populous countries in the region. Turkish is the official language, but many people also speak English, especially in tourist areas. The country's capital is Ankara, though Istanbul is the largest and most culturally significant city.

Turkey has a rich and diverse history, with the ancient city of Troy being one of its most famous historical sites. The country was home to several ancient civilizations, including the Greeks, Romans, and Byzantines, and was later the heart of the Ottoman Empire, which lasted for over 600 years. Today, Turkey is a modern republic that has maintained its historical charm through its unique landmarks, ancient ruins, and vibrant cultural traditions. Visitors flock to Turkey to experience its renowned cuisine, rich history, and stunning landscapes, from the surreal fairy chimneys of Cappadocia to the Mediterranean beaches.

Fun Trivia About Turkey

Home to Two Continents: Turkey is the only country in the world that spans two continents, Europe and Asia. The Bosporus Strait separates the two, and Istanbul, Turkey's largest city, is the only city in the world to be located on two continents.

World's Oldest Temple: The world's oldest known temple, Gabelli Tepe, is located in Turkey's southeastern Anatolia region. It dates back to around 9600 BCE, predating Stonehenge by thousands of years.

Turkish Delight: The sweet treat known as Turkish delight (locum) originated in Turkey. It's made from sugar, starch, and various flavorings, and has been enjoyed since the 15th century.

Mount Ararat: Turkey is home to Mount Ararat, the tallest mountain in the country and the legendary resting place of Noah's Ark according to the Bible.

Cappadocia's Fairy Chimneys: The rock formations in Cappadocia, often referred to as fairy chimneys, are formed by volcanic eruptions and centuries of erosion. Visitors can explore them through hiking, hot air ballooning, and cave dwellings.

Turkish Baths (Hammams): Traditional Turkish baths, or hammams, are an ancient form of steam bath used for relaxation and purification. They have been a part of Turkish culture for centuries and remain a popular experience for tourists.

Rich Culinary Heritage: Turkey's culinary scene is a mixture of various cultures and regions. Dishes like kebabs, mezes, baklava, and Turkish tea are beloved staples. The country's diverse landscapes and climates influence its cooking, providing a rich variety of flavors from coast to coast.

Turkey's combination of history, culture, and unique natural wonders makes it an intriguing destination for travelers worldwide. Whether exploring its ancient ruins, enjoying its food, or marveling at its landscapes, Turkey offers an experience that is both diverse and unforgettable.

CONCLUSION

The Journey, The Discovery, The Adventure

"Every ending is just the beginning of a new adventure. The story may end here, but the journey continues within you."

As we reach the end of this journey, I find myself reflecting on how much we've explored together. Whether you've just turned the first page or you've been following the twists and turns from the beginning, this book has been a voyage — not just through words and ideas, but through the heart and soul of the story we've shared. It's been an adventure, hasn't it?

We've navigated the complexities, taken some unexpected detours, and laughed (and maybe even shed a tear) along the way. But isn't that what makes any journey memorable? It's not just about the destination, but the experiences we collect along the way, the people we meet, and the lessons we learn that shape us into who we're meant to be.

As you read these final lines, I want to ask you: What did you discover? What part of this book made you pause, think, or feel something unexpected? Perhaps it was a character's resilience, an insight you hadn't considered before, or maybe it was just the feeling of being lost in a world that felt as real as your own. This, my friend, is the beauty of storytelling — the ability to transport us, challenge us, and ultimately change us.

Every chapter we've ventured through represents a piece of something larger. And, as in any good story, the ending is just another beginning. The themes explored within these pages aren't limited to the confines of the chapters; they extend far beyond, into your life, your world, and the future that you'll shape with the knowledge and emotions you've gained here.

Now, you may be wondering, "What comes next?" While I don't have all the answers, I do know that the final page isn't the end of this adventure. Rather, it's an invitation to carry forward the story, the lessons, and the energy from this book into your own life. The ideas explored here aren't just confined to words on paper—

they're seeds planted in your mind, waiting to grow, evolve, and transform in ways that may surprise you.

Take what you've learned and apply it. Let it inspire you to look at the world with new eyes. Maybe you'll be bolder in your choices, kinder in your actions, or more determined in pursuing your dreams. Whatever it is, let the echoes of this journey resonate with you long after the last page is turned.

In the end, this book is not just a finished product, but a conversation we've started. So, if you feel compelled to share your thoughts, your feedback, or your own story, I encourage you to do so. We're all part of this grand narrative, each contributing our own chapter, our own voice, our own perspective.

To those who have laughed, cried, and even grown frustrated alongside the characters, thank you for traveling this road with me. Your investment in this book has meant more than just reading; it's been an act of engagement, of curiosity, and of connection. And I can't help but believe that the journey we've shared will stay with you in some way.

As you close this book, remember: the world is vast, your potential is limitless, and the story is far from over. This may be the end of one chapter, but it's the beginning of countless others that are just waiting to be written. You are the author of your own life, and there's so much more waiting for you beyond the final sentence.

So, what will your next chapter be? Will you take the lessons from this book and apply them to your own journey? Will you step into the unknown with the confidence you've gained? Whatever path you choose, I know one thing is certain — your story will be just as extraordinary as the one we've shared here.

THANK YOU FOR BEING PART OF THIS ADVENTURE. UNTIL THE NEXT STORY, MAY YOUR LIFE BE FULL OF DISCOVERY, GROWTH, AND ENDLESS POSSIBILITY. THE WORLD IS WAITING FOR YOU, AND THE BEST IS YET TO COME.

Made in United States
Orlando, FL
31 May 2025

61728636R00115